Contents

Chapter 7   Exam skills

Exam board focus

AIMING FOR AN A IN A-LEVEL HISTORY

Nicholas Fellows

HODDER
EDUCATION
AN HACHETTE UK COMPANY

Acknowledgements

With thanks to the CDARE team at the Sheffield Institute of Education for their assistance developing and reviewing this title.

Every effort has been made to trace all copyright holders, but if any have been inadvertently overlooked, the Publishers will be pleased to make the necessary arrangements at the first opportunity.

Although every effort has been made to ensure that website addresses are correct at time of going to press, Hodder Education cannot be held responsible for the content of any website mentioned in this book. It is sometimes possible to find a relocated web page by typing in the address of the home page for a website in the URL window of your browser.

Hachette UK's policy is to use papers that are natural, renewable and recyclable products and made from wood grown in sustainable forests. The logging and manufacturing processes are expected to conform to the environmental regulations of the country of origin.

Orders: please contact Bookpoint Ltd, 130 Park Drive, Milton Park, Abingdon, Oxon OX14 4SE. Telephone: (44) 01235 827827. Fax: (44) 01235 400401. Email education@bookpoint.co.uk Lines are open from 9 a.m. to 5 p.m., Monday to Saturday, with a 24-hour message answering service. You can also order through our website: www.hoddereducation.co.uk

ISBN: 978 1 5104 2923 9

First published in 2018 by

Hodder Education,

An Hachette UK Company

Carmelite House

50 Victoria Embankment

London EC4Y 0DZ

www.hoddereducation.co.uk

Impression number   10 9 8 7 6 5 4 3 2 1

Year   2021 2020 2019 2018

Typeset by Integra Software Services Pvt. Ltd., Pondicherry, India

Printed in Spain

A catalogue record for this title is available from the British Library.

Getting the most from this book

Aiming for an A is designed to help you master the skills you need to achieve the highest grades.
The following features will help you get the most from this book.

Learning objectives

> A summary of the skills that will be covered in the chapter.

Exam tip

Practical advice about how to apply your skills to the exam.

Activity

An opportunity to test your skills with practical activities.

! Common pitfall

Problem areas where candidates often miss out on marks.

The difference between...

Key concepts differentiated and explained.

Annotated example

Exemplar answers with commentary showing how to achieve top grades.

Take it further

Suggestions for further reading or activities that will stretch your thinking.

You should know

> A summary of key points to take away from the chapter.

About this book

Although history is about the past, it is about a past that is still alive and influencing our lives today, making it both relevant and fascinating — and not, as Henry Ford said, 'more or less bunk'. With historians constantly reinterpreting the past, our understanding of it is constantly changing.

You will have chosen to study the subject at A-level for many possible reasons. You may have an interest in the history of a particular country, period or person or you may simply have an interest in the past. Whatever period you study, there should be plenty to captivate you and encourage you to take your study beyond the classroom. You may not know much about the period you are going to study, but that will have little impact on your final grade. What will matter is **how you approach your study.** Your willingness to apply yourself and develop your study skills will play a major role in determining your final grade. That is where this book can help you.

The aim of this book is to identify and develop the skills that are necessary to achieve a top grade in history. The various chapters will help you develop the key skills you need to succeed, such as reading, note-taking and essay writing. Their development will play a key role in ensuring you achieve a high grade in your final examination. The skills will be developed over the whole 2 years (or 1 if you are doing AS) of your study. So this book is not simply a revision guide, to be read in those last few weeks before the examination, when it will actually be too late. Instead, it needs to be used constantly throughout your course.

Your approach

You will soon discover that life in the sixth form is very different to your other years at school. Studying will be **more independent**, and you will be set work that may not need to be completed for the next lesson or even the next week. You may be given lists of books that you could read to help with a topic or from which you could take notes. In other words, you may find your time far less structured and organised by your teachers than you have been accustomed to. This will put a greater emphasis on your own efforts and therefore much of what you achieve will depend on you and how you approach your study.

The purpose of this book is to help you in this process, which can at first appear quite daunting and challenging. This book should become a trusted friend. It may not tell you what to read or what to write for a particular essay, but it will explain how to go about the tasks and **improve the skills that are essential for success**. You are more likely to succeed if, from the very start of your A-level course, you are well organised, know the requirements of your examination board and have a positive outlook towards your work. This book should go some way in helping you to improve your marks during your course of study. However, most of the improvement will ultimately depend on you and your attitude.

Without a **positive attitude** and a passion for your subject it is much harder to improve. There are no shortcuts to success and hard work is essential — but with a positive attitude and use of this book you will get the maximum benefit from the time you put into your work. This book will offer you plenty of advice, but it is up to you to put it into practice.

There is a quote from a famous South African golfer, Gary Player, which is worth remembering when times get hard: 'Strange, the harder I practise the better I seem to get!' So keep going and keep applying yourself.

Take it further

Construct a chart that shows each day of the week. Break it down into half-hour slots and colour code each slot according to lessons, study time, activities, social time, eating and sleeping time. Use this chart to see where you could make better use of your time to improve your work.

You will need to buy into the learning process. When you get a piece of marked work back, don't just look at the mark and file it away or compare it with your friend's and think 'Great, I beat them!' The comments at the end of the work and the marginal comments are much more important than the final mark. If you read the comments carefully and try to apply them to your next piece of work, then the chances are that you will improve, just like Gary Player. The essays you write at the start of the course will not be as good as those at the end — if they were, why would you wait a year or 2 years to do the exam?

So don't give up. Improvement is not always quick, but remember that the essays you do in class or at home are simply practice for the final examination and in the end it is how you perform in that which really matters. Use the advice in this book and the feedback on your work to help you keep going and you will see progress.

General advice

Before we look at each of the skills that you will need to develop, there is some generic advice that should form the basis of all your A-level study:

→ **In some subjects there might be a 'right answer'**, but this is not the case in history and many examination board mark schemes acknowledge this by stating that 'no set answer is expected'. It depends how you, just like historians, interpret the evidence. Provided you can support your view with accurate evidence that is fine.

→ **There is also no set 'formula' for essay writing.** It is important that you develop your own style. Obviously within that you will need to demonstrate a clear, consistent and supported argument that leads to a supported judgement. Developing your own style will allow you to write with passion and this usually leads to the best responses.

→ **This is not GCSE** where you could often do well by simply learning material. At AS and A-level you will need to show understanding and a greater ability to analyse and evaluate material.

→ **Make sure you know the demands of the examination board** for which you are studying. Be clear about the mark schemes and what is required for each of the level descriptors. Once you know what is required it is easier to set out to achieve it.

→ **Pay careful attention to the comments on your work**; use them and this book to help you reach the next level.

→ **It is a considerable jump from GCSE to A-level**, so do not expect your first essay to be outstanding. It will take time to develop the skills necessary for a top A-level grade — remember you have 2 years to get there.

→ **If you want to improve your written work then read.** Reading will not only give you ideas and different views, but will help you develop a better writing style.

→ **Use every available resource.** Read articles in journals, watch television programmes, go to lectures, use the library, talk to other students and swap essays. Ensure that you use the examination board's website. Remember that your teacher is there to help and support you — do ask for guidance.

Take it further

Check the daily listings for television programmes not just on your topics of study, but for history in general. They may inspire you and provide a prompt or an area of interest that could possibly be pursued when you do your coursework.

→ **Use the internet**, but ensure that the sites you use can be trusted and avoid the sites that offer essay-writing help. Many give very bad advice and you need to develop your own style with which you are comfortable.

However, the best advice is to enjoy the subject. There may be parts of the course that are less enjoyable, but find something you really enjoy and develop it — this will help you when you find other parts less stimulating. Once you are enjoying the work you will be surprised how much progress you make. You may even become so engrossed in it that time passes quickly and you forget to do other things. Engage with it, talk about it and you will be surprised how much you get back and how it helps you improve.

How to use this book

We have already said that this book is not simply for use when you start revising, but should be in your bag along with your notes and books for the whole course. There is information in it that you will need on a daily basis if you are to make the progress you want.

The book will take you through the skills you need from the first day of your course to the final exam and provide you with the guidance you need for success.

→ First, **Chapter 1** will discuss the purpose of the history exam and the skills that it assesses, and will provide advice on organising your study time.

→ In **Chapter 2** you will learn how to read for a purpose and take notes that are useful for writing a class essay and for providing you with information which you can use to revise.

→ In **Chapter 3** you will be guided through the stages of writing a good A-level essay, from the planning stage to the conclusion. This will ensure that, by the time you come to the final exam, you have mastered a skill that will have great bearing on your overall performance.

→ In **Chapter 4** you will develop the skills you need to work with both primary and secondary sources, that other integral part of your exam.

→ In **Chapter 5** coursework or the extended essay will be explained so that you can get started promptly and address the key skills that are being tested.

→ **Chapter 6** will examine skills that are specific to the OCR examination board, for the short essay and the thematic essay, ensuring that all areas of your final assessment are covered.

→ Following this coverage of all the elements that make up your exam, **Chapter 7** will give you guidance on how to maximise your efforts in preparing for that crucial exam.

→ Finally, the **Exam board focus** section gives information about each of the exam boards so you can see how the assessment works and what skills are assessed for your particular board.

Therefore, provided you use this book regularly, it will give you the detailed guidance you need to show the examiner the skills required to reach the very top. Good luck with your studies and hopefully they will be both worthwhile and enjoyable.

1 Your history exam

The purpose of the exam

Examinations are not particularly enjoyable and you may suffer from nerves, but by being well prepared you can go at least part of the way to overcoming that.

It will also help you achieve your best if you can try and look at exams as something other than 'tests' or an attempt to try and trick you — believe it or not, that is not the aim of examiners. You will do much better if you can see the exam as the chance to show what you can do — after all, that is why you have spent the time studying the subject. This might seem a strange way to view an exam, but the better prepared you are the more likelihood there is of this happening. That means you will need to have revised thoroughly. This does not mean simply staring at your notes for a long time trying to absorb everything on the page, but undertaking active revision, as will be seen in Chapter 7.

The examination is not simply about recalling a list of facts — no exam will ask you to write all you know about a subject, although many students do. Instead it will **test a number of skills** that you have developed over the course. The knowledge that you have gained will need to be used to support an argument or to test the view in either a primary source or an interpretation.

In **source questions** you will have to comprehend what the source is saying about the issue in the question. You will need to test what the source says against your knowledge of the period to see if the view offered in the source is valid. You will also need to think about whether the validity is reduced or improved by considering its provenance — who wrote it, when they wrote it and why they wrote it.

In the **interpretation questions** you will again need to comprehend the text and be able to explain its view about the issue in the question. You will need to test the view in the interpretation by comparing it with your knowledge of the period and issue.

In the **essay questions** you will need to analyse a range of issues or factors. You will have to explore and analyse both sides of the argument to reach a balanced conclusion; if you just describe the arguments or consider only one side you will not do as well. You should aim to show a supported judgement for each issue you have discussed and reach an overall judgement.

The examination boards also require you to do a piece of **coursework**, that is an extended piece of writing, usually between 3,000 and 4,000 words in length. The skills tested by this vary among examination boards, as does the nature of the question you undertake, so make sure you follow the requirements for your examination board. The number of words is not very large, but do not leave it to the last minute — allow sufficient time to write a convincing answer that meets all the criteria of the examination board. Create a schedule and keep to it, giving yourself time to find the sources and books you need. Make sure you understand the demands of the question you are answering and focus on meeting these demands.

> ## ! Common pitfall
>
> One of the biggest failures of candidates is the failure to answer the question they have been set. You have time to check your coursework, so make sure that you have not simply described events, that you have remained focused on the actual question and that you have used the type of sources your examination board requires.

> ## ! Common pitfall
>
> Avoid trying to just memorise your notes. Active revision is much more productive than just sitting staring at your notes and trying to absorb all the information on the page. If you try to do the latter, you will find you lose concentration after about 5 minutes and your time will not be used productively. Instead you need 'to do'. That means making summaries of your notes, making plans for past questions using your notes, testing yourself by making plans without notes, making lists of reasons and checking them against your notes — in fact almost anything other than just trying to learn your notes by rote.

> ## Take it further
>
> In order to achieve the best possible result, ensure you know which examination board's specification you are following and which papers you are studying within that specification. Each examination board has its own website and you will be able to find the specification there as well as past papers, mark schemes and possibly sample answers. It is a good idea to become familiar with these as they will be what you are judged against.

The examiner

Teachers will at some stage make a comment about 'the examiner', that is the person who will mark your examination paper. Although you do not need to know a great deal about the examiner, it is probably helpful to be aware that most examiners are teachers, just like the person who has prepared you for the exam. They are not ogres who get pleasure from awarding a low mark and take every opportunity to deduct marks rather than give credit for what you have actually done.

Not only will the examiner have the necessary subject knowledge about the topics they are marking, but they will also have had to undergo training and be approved as an examiner before they can mark 'live' examination papers such as yours. During their training they will have been made aware of a range of possible ways of answering questions and instructed that there is no such thing as a right or wrong way of answering a question. Their attention will have been drawn to a phrase that is present in many mark schemes that '**no set answer is required**'. They will also have been told that if they come across an unexpected answer they should consult with a more senior examiner on how to apply the mark scheme.

The examiner will have worked through a range of practice scripts so that they know the standard for each level and can apply it in the same way that the senior examiner will. Examiners will have been told that their job is to apply the mark scheme by asking what level best describes your answer, crediting all material that is relevant regardless of whether it appears in the mark scheme. It is also worth remembering that when the examination questions are set, the aim is not to try and 'catch you out', but rather to see what you know and how you can use your knowledge. All of this should give you confidence in the process; every examiner wants to make sure that your work gets the mark it deserves.

There are also ways in which you can help the examiner:

→ Do try to write legibly. It is a good idea to handwrite as many of your class and practice essays as possible so that you get accustomed to handwriting, particularly under timed conditions, before you do the examination.

→ Do number the questions correctly. If you do that, there is no need to write out the question, although it may help you to remain focused on the actual question.

→ Avoid writing in the margins, particularly writing sideways. This will be very difficult to read, as exam scripts are usually scanned in.

→ Try to avoid adding material after you have written a paragraph; if you do need to add material, provide clear labels to show where it should go. Lots of stars and asterisks can make it difficult for an examiner to follow an answer.

→ If you miss a page out in the exam booklet and later realise you have done this, do put a note to the examiner to 'turn over' to ensure they are aware that you have not finished.

→ If you use extra answer booklets, do number them clearly so that they get scanned in in the correct order.

Assessment objectives and levels

In the examination your work will be marked against a generic mark scheme and it is important that you understand how you will be assessed in the exam. Understanding the mark scheme will help you focus on the particular skills you need to develop in order to target the higher levels. Assessment objectives (or AOs) are, as the name suggests, the objectives against which your work will be marked (assessed).

All the examination boards use the same assessment objectives, even if they are not given the same weight. The Exam board focus section will provide you with specific information on your examination board.

> **! Common pitfall**
>
> Avoid running out of time in the examination. Be aware from the very start how long you will have for each type of question and stick to these times.

> **! Common pitfall**
>
> Do be careful what pen you use in the exam. Ensure that you have used it before and that it will not cause blotches or go through the page as this will cause problems when the script is scanned and make it much harder for the examiner to read. Do use black ink as that scans much better.

Assessment objective 1 (AO1)

'Demonstrate, organise and communicate knowledge and understanding to analyse and evaluate the key features related to the periods studied, making substantiated judgements and exploring concepts, as relevant, of cause, consequence, change, continuity, similarity, difference and significance.'

This assessment objective is about what you know, but it is not just about describing events and issues. As mentioned earlier, just learning facts is not what is needed — you must be able to analyse and evaluate them. That means you will gain little credit if you just describe how Hitler came to power or how Henry VIII broke from Rome; instead you will need to be able to explain a range of reasons for these events and, to get to the very top, be able to evaluate them. The word 'evaluate' is very important; in this context it means to give a value or weight to each of the reasons, so that you have explained their relative importance.

What is **analysis**? At a very basic level, analysis involves taking apart an issue and explaining how it works, and how it links to the question you have been asked. It is important to break down the 'point' of your paragraph so that you use your information to link it back to the question.

What's the difference between **describing** and **explaining**? A descriptive account will tell the story of what happened. You will simply give an account of events. However, with explanation you will show how an issue or range of issues brought about an event, linking the account to the reason or justification for the event.

What is **evaluation**? If you look closely at the word you can probably work out for yourself what it means. You are giving a value to each issue or factor. In doing this you are deciding which factor is the most important, which factors are of lesser importance and why, and justifying your decision by using your knowledge to support it.

It will be of little value just learning a lot of details as no question will ask you to write all you know about Henry VIII, Hitler or Stalin. Instead you will need to select material that is relevant to the actual question set. In relating the material to the question you will show that you not only know the information but also understand it and are able to use it.

In order to show a clear line of argument it is helpful to set it out in the opening paragraph and then argue your point using evidence and showing why other arguments are less valid. This type of approach will ensure that you evaluate the issues and reach a supported judgement in your conclusion.

Assessment objective 2 (AO2)

'Analyse and evaluate appropriate source material, primary and/ or contemporary to the period, within its historical context.'

This assessment objective is about the analysis of primary sources, that is sources that were written at the time of an event or close to that time, considering the utility of a source for a particular purpose and assessing the validity of the view the source offers about an issue. In simple terms this means assessing how far you

✓ **Exam tip**

Many candidates think that the more they write and the more points or issues they cover, the more marks they will score. This is not true. The answers that score the highest marks are consistently analytical. In these responses the factors or issues are broken down, discussed and linked back to the question. Furthermore, these factors or issues are evaluated, not just listed.

✓ **Exam tip**

It is best to avoid phrases such as 'Another factor' which give the impression that you are just listing reasons. Do not expect to cover every issue in an examination essay, as you won't have time. Include only the points you think are most important.

✓ **Exam tip**

Ensure that you explain the source's view about the issue in the question and then use both contextual knowledge and a consideration of the provenance of a primary source when you evaluate it.

can trust what the source is saying. This may be done by considering the provenance of the source and by testing its content against your knowledge, to see whether the source agrees or disagrees with what you know to be the case.

Annotated example: analysing a source

This example shows the type of approach you could adopt when analysing a source. It shows part of an answer to the question below. (The sources are not shown here. You will find more detailed guidance on working with sources in Chapter 4.)

Using these sources, assess the view that the restoration of Catholicism under Mary enjoyed little popular support.

The source is explained and the view of the source about the issue in the question is stated.

The reliability of Parkyn's view is raised as an issue, so the provenance of the source is considered.

Source A argues that not only was the restoration of Catholicism quick, but it was also popular as 'the English service was voluntarily laid aside and the Latin taken up again, and all without compulsion'. Not only that, but all the old ceremonies were being used by the end of 1554 — just over a year after Mary's accession. Parkyn's account is based on the north of England, where Catholicism had traditionally been strong, as was seen in the reaction to the closure of the smaller monasteries in 1536 and to the formula of wills under both Henry and Edward. However, there is some evidence that suggests this account was not untypical even though Parkyn was a firm supporter of Catholicism: in Melton Mowbray, a small Midlands town, the bells were rung to greet Mary's accession; and in Parliament, a mass was said voluntarily before the law had been changed to enforce its use.

The source is evaluated with both consideration of its provenance and use of detailed contextual knowledge to show that, despite Parkyn being a strong Catholic, the provenance does not undermine the view.

Assessment objective 3 (AO3)

'Analyse and evaluate, in relation to the historical context, different ways in which aspects of the past have been interpreted.'

This assessment objective is about the different interpretations of the past that historians have constructed, in other words secondary sources. You will need to understand how historians have explained the events you have studied and be able to assess the strengths and limitations of those interpretations. This is best done by using your contextual knowledge to test the views: think about what knowledge you have that either agrees with the view they are offering or challenges it. Then link that knowledge to the interpretation using

✓ Exam tip

It is a good idea to build up a list of evaluative words during your course of study; you might start with the two basic ones of 'right' and 'wrong'.

evaluative words, such as 'valid', 'weak', 'challenges', 'however', 'indeed' or 'moreover'. This might take the form of 'The view of Jones about the Russian Revolution is valid because...', where you then bring in your own knowledge to support what Jones has said. On the other hand, you might argue that 'The view of Jones that the Russian Revolution of October 1917 was a popular event can be challenged by...' and then bring in your knowledge that challenges the view.

Assessment levels

When marking your work, the first thing an examiner will have been told to do is work out which level it best fits. They will look back at the annotations they have made in the margins to determine which skills you have shown and use this to inform their judgement. They will be aware of key words and phrases.

Next the examiner will think about whether you have demonstrated all the skills needed for that level. If you have, they will consider whether there is anything to take you into the next level up, or whether you are at the top of that level. If you have covered most of the requirements they will place you in the middle and if you have just shown some of the requirements you will be at the lower end of the level.

Getting organised for study

You will soon discover that, whatever subjects you are studying, A-levels require much more independent work than was the case for GCSEs or IGCSEs. You will be set work for a week's time or sometimes even a fortnight's time and this will require you to plan your time and be organised. You will not be able to do all the work the night before it is due in, and anyway you will need time to think and reflect before writing major pieces of work.

There are a number of basic things that you can do to help yourself:

→ Ensure that you have some files, preferably one to keep current work in and then a larger, lever-arch file to store work when you have finished a topic. Don't carry all your work round with you just in case it goes missing.

→ Use dividers to help you keep your work organised. This will be particularly useful when it comes to finding notes for an essay or when you start revising. It is helpful to divide your work up according to the topics or study areas in the specification.

→ Use file paper rather than an exercise book for taking notes. It is more useful as additional notes on a topic can be slotted into your file at the correct place rather than appearing out of sequence in a notebook. File paper will also make it much easier for you to organise your notes.

→ Follow the advice given in the next chapter on how to take and organise your notes. It is far better to have a set of organised notes when it comes to writing an essay or revising than to be forced to spend a few hours of precious time searching for notes you cannot find.

→ Run a homework diary electronically or in hard copy in a diary. Write down work as it is set and note when it is due in. You will not be studying just history and therefore will have to organise the work for your other subjects as well.

→ If you take notes on a computer do ensure you back them up. It is distressing to discover that the memory stick on which you have saved them has become corrupt or something has happened to the hard drive.

Get organised from the very start. It is far easier to establish a working routine at the outset than to have to suddenly implement one halfway through your study when it may be too late and you have lost valuable time.

> ✓ **Exam tip**
>
> Being organised will mean that you make good use of your available time. Instead of looking for missing work you can spend that hour doing further reading which is likely to enhance your grade.

You should know

> A01 is about knowledge, understanding and analysis; A02 is about the analysis and evaluation of primary or contemporary sources; and A03 is about the analysis and evaluation of different interpretations of the past. In order to do well you will need to show a command of all three assessment objectives.

> There is some overlap between analysis and evaluation, but evaluation also requires you to give a 'value' to a source, interpretation, factor or issue.

> In handling primary sources it is important to be aware of their provenance and the historical context in which they were written.

> In handling interpretations you will need to be able to explain them and test the views expressed by using your knowledge of the period.

> Some questions cover longer periods than others and you may need to compare events or issues across the period.

> It is important to be organised from the very start of your course.

2 Reading and note-taking

Learning objectives

> To be able to employ a range of reading strategies and know when to use the different types
> To know how to take notes effectively for writing essays and for revision purposes

Reading will play a crucial role in your studying: not only will it help you develop a better understanding of the period and issues that you will be examined on, but it will also help you develop your essay-writing skills. You may think that you already now how to read, but there is a big difference between reading and reading effectively, with the latter being a much more difficult skill to master.

Reading will be vital in providing you with a wider range of ideas and evidence than can ever be covered in the classroom. It will keep you up to date with current research on your topics of study and hopefully enthuse you with new ideas and approaches. In particular, it will be crucial when it comes to coursework and independent research, where you will need a range of reading skills.

There is a considerable difference between passive and active reading, as shown in the box below.

The difference between...

Passive reading	Active reading
• Brings little benefit • Unlikely that you will remember much of what you have read • Unlikely that you will be able to relate it to what you are studying	• Reading for a purpose • Discovering what the writer's view is about events • Understanding how they interpret an issue • Understanding how they support their argument

If you are reading to answer actual questions, rather than just reading about the topic, you are much more likely to take the material in and remember it.

Types of reading

There are three main types of active reading that you will need to master to be successful at history. They are:

→ skim-reading
→ scan-reading
→ critical reading

Aiming for an A in A-level History

All of these types of reading will be important in developing your skills for AO1 by building your knowledge and understanding. However, it is important to know what you are trying to achieve before you start reading as otherwise you could spend a great deal of time for very little gain. It might be helpful to think of these three types of reading as stages in your reading.

Skim-reading

Skim-reading is the process by which you find out whether what you are reading is actually relevant to what you are studying. You are looking to see if what the text is saying is relevant and to decide whether it is worth reading more carefully.

To do this you can:
→ look for relevant headings and subheadings
→ look for key words
→ look at the opening paragraph of a section
→ look at the opening sentences of each paragraph

You may decide that some paragraphs are worth further reading and others are not. By doing this you will not waste time reading material that is not relevant.

Scan-reading

You have identified that the piece is worth reading more carefully and now you are looking for specific information or evidence, perhaps about why an event happened. You may not need to read the whole of the piece: if it includes description of events about which you already have notes and are confident, it would not be worthwhile to read those parts. Instead, you can do scan-reading, going through the piece to look for the particular information you want.

Such an approach will keep you focused and stop you from drifting. It will also ensure that you do not take repetitive notes about an event which you have already covered in your notes — you do not have the time for that.

Critical reading

Having carried out your initial reading to find out what happened, usually at the very start of a topic when you need to get a basic overview or narrative from your textbook, you should have a secure knowledge of events. You are then ready to move on to what is called 'critical reading'. This type of active reading is done to find out what the writer's view is about an issue and what evidence they use to support it. Once again, you will need to take notes, summarising the view and bullet-pointing the evidence used to support the argument.

Take it further

Construct a summary chart for a history book you are using, with a column for each of the key questions you need to ask yourself while reading. Fill in each column and then use the information to write a summary of the argument and how far you agree with it.

In this instance you will be asking yourself a number of key questions as you read:

→ What is the writer saying?

→ What evidence does the writer put forward to support his or her view?

→ What do I know that either supports or challenges the view of the writer?

→ In light of my knowledge, can I trust the writer's view?

→ Is the view of the writer surprising or unexpected?

Activity

Read the following paragraph on the importance of terror in the maintenance of Nazi support, and consider the question below.

Extract 1

Once the threat from the political left had been eliminated, from the mid 1930s, the Nazi terror began to concentrate on silencing potential sources of opposition in religious circles and on removing from society what the regime deemed social outsiders, such as homosexuals, career criminals and the physically and mentally disabled. During the war the terror reached its most dramatic phase. Although many German citizens belonged to one or more of the targeted groups, most Germans suffered not at all from terror. There was no need to target them because most Germans remained loyal to the Nazi leadership and supported it voluntarily from the beginning to the end, to various degrees. Some Germans voluntarily spied on and denounced their neighbours, but the overwhelming majority of German citizens did not. It remains true, however, that the German civilian population played a large part in its own control and its collusion and accommodation with the Nazi regime made the Nazi crimes against humanity possible.

(Source: Eric Johnson, *The Nazi Terror*, Basic Books, 1999)

Question

What is Johnson's argument about the role of terror in maintaining Nazi support?

You might also take this a stage further and consider how far you agree with Johnson's view. What do you know that either agrees or disagrees with his view? This will allow you to take a critical view of his interpretation, which will be particularly useful when it comes to an essay on how Hitler maintained power and will also help you develop a useful skill for AO3, which is discussed further in Chapter 4.

The paragraph above may not provide you with the evidence that Johnson uses to support his argument and you may need to read on to find that, but you can do that by scan-reading.

What to read

Many of the books and articles you read will have been specifically written for A-level students and therefore the language will be accessible. However, if you are aiming to develop your understanding further, which is essential for the top grades, or to find material for your coursework, then you will need to look at more academic books and journals where you will come across more complex arguments and language.

Take it further

Check to see if your school or local library has subscriptions to magazines such as *History Today*, *Modern History* Review and *BBC History*. Make it a habit each month to identify and read those articles relevant to each topic you are studying.

Take, for example, the paragraph from Eric Johnson quoted above. Note that what he says at the start of the paragraph, which suggests terror was important, is not actually his main argument, which is developed only in the second half of the paragraph. You will therefore need to take care with such work — in this instance a book that looks at the work of the Gestapo in one German town, Krefeld — and ensure that you identify the argument correctly.

You will also come across concepts and vocabulary that are more challenging. Do not just ignore this — look up words and concepts, and ask your teacher if you need more help. There can be a great sense of achievement in grappling with a difficult passage and working out what is being argued and why.

A reading hierarchy

You will soon discover that you cannot make much progress with your history studies unless you are willing to read. Teachers will set you material to read and if you want to reach those higher grades you will need to read widely. The problem is more likely to be knowing what to read. Your teacher may give you a list of books, and you can also go and find material yourself. However, there is a range of books out there on the topic or topics that you are studying and it is advisable to approach your reading in a structured way. Think of it as moving up a reading hierarchy from introductory overview to more advanced, in-depth materials.

The best place to start will be your textbook or topic book which your teacher will probably have given you. This will provide you with an introduction to, or a survey of, the topic and allow you to gain a basic understanding before you go and read more complex material. It will give you a chronological overview and probably introduce you to the basic debates that surround the topic.

Take it further

Construct your own reading list for each topic you are studying. Create a hierarchy starting with the relevant pages from your textbook, then move on to topic books, journals, and finally more specialist texts.

Your textbook

Your textbook may have been written specifically for your course and will be accessible and accurate. If it is written specifically for your course then it will focus on the specification and the issues on which exam questions are most likely to be set. It may also provide you with further reading lists and even comment on the accessibility and suitability of the books, which can be very helpful.

Topic books

Topic books will go into more detail than your textbook and may still be written for A-level students or university students and therefore be accessible. They will develop some of the issues raised in the textbook and provide you with greater depth of support.

Articles in journals for students

Some publishers produce history journals aimed specifically at students in sixth form, for example *Moden History Review* published by Hodder Education. These again are likely to be accessible and are particularly valuable in keeping you up to date on recent research and developments in your topic.

Further reading

Further reading will involve you tackling specialist books, such as that by Eric Johnson. These will be more challenging, and the arguments may be more nuanced and subtle. This kind of reading should not be tackled until you have a firm grasp of the topic and an awareness of the debates.

When you are ready to approach a specialist work, it is often a good idea to read the introduction and conclusion first. These should give a clear idea of the argument that the author is going to pursue in the book and (after discussion of their research) a summary of their view, probably placing it in the wider context of the debate, which is particularly useful. This will help you to find the arguments you are looking for and then identify the support the author uses to back up their point of view.

You will often find that journals have articles written by these authors in which they explain their views in a more condensed form. In many instances this can be much easier, but do not shy away from the more academic books as you may find you need them for your coursework (see Chapter 5).

> **! Common pitfall**
>
> If you went to a specialist book first, you would not have the contextual knowledge or awareness of the debates needed to make sense of the arguments and you would therefore not gain the maximum benefit from reading it.

Note-taking

Why take notes?

Your notes will be crucial to you throughout your course. They will form the basis of the essays that you write during the course and you will use them to revise from when you are preparing for your examination. So take care of them, keep them organised and do not lose them.

Although it might sound obvious, ensure that your notes are genuine notes and that, if you are taking notes from a book, you do not copy out large sections of the book. The main reason for taking notes from a book is so that you do not need to go back to the book at a later date. If you do need to go back to the book, your original notes were not doing their job. You will need to achieve a balance to ensure that you have sufficient depth to allow you to support an argument, but not so much detail that you are swamped and cannot see the argument.

Developing your own style of note-taking is also important. You will develop your own shorthand, a system of headings and subheadings, and a style of page layout.

> **! Common pitfall**
>
> Ensure your notes are genuine notes and you do not simply copy out large sections of the book from which you are working.

Do not worry if most of the page on which you have made notes i[s] blank. There is nothing harder to revise from than a side of dense written text. That looks just like a textbook, whereas notes shou[ld] be a summary of the lesson, lecture, book or article you have attended or used.

What notes should I take?

There are a number of different reasons for taking notes and different types of notes. Obviously you will need to note dow[n] important things during a lesson or from your reading. These [will] include:

→ an outline or chronology of the topic you are studying

→ any key debates and interpretations associated with the top[ic]

→ evidence to support the different views and interpretations

→ any questions that you have about an issue

→ new evidence and ideas that relate to issues you are studying

This should tell you that you do not need to note down everything. It is a major pitfall for students to try and write everything down in a lesson or from a book, with the result that they have pages of notes they will never use or, having read a range of books or articles on a topic, they have written down the same thing a number of times.

In short, you should ensure that:

→ you have a clear chronology of the events

→ you have explained each event

→ you are aware of the significance of each event

→ you note down only events that are relevant to your course

→ you do not note down the same thing more than once

If you have taken good notes you will not need to return to a book or article, but if you want to quote the views of a particular historian you have read or use some of their evidence to support your ideas then it is helpful to have the following information:

→ the name of the author

→ the title of the book or article

→ the relevant page in the book or article — this can be noted in the margin

→ the date the book was published

Noting these details is also a good habit to develop as you will need to acknowledge your sources of information in longer essays, for example in your coursework, or later at university.

How to take notes

Notes are very personal and it is crucial that you develop your own style, regardless of whether you take notes on paper or on a computer. Many students like to highlight selected text in articles they are given, but in doing this it is less likely that you will remember the main points of the article or will revisit it when you are revising — it is better to take notes.

> **! Common pitfall**
>
> Do not try and write down everything in a lesson or lecture — remember notes are summaries. You may already have some of the information and there is no point in writing it down again.

While notes are personal to you as the only one who will use them and need to understand them, there are some important points to remember:

→ Do not copy out large amounts of text. You need to put the material into your own words so that you are certain you understand it, and you will not remember large amounts of information you have just copied out.

→ Notes should be more than just a narrative of events. Once you have noted the narrative, ensure that further notes consider arguments and the evidence that supports them.

→ Develop your own shorthand — some obvious examples are 'HVIII' (for Henry VIII) or 'Parl' (Parliament).

→ Use bullet points, arrows, lists and charts.

→ Use headings and subheadings, perhaps using different colours to distinguish them.

→ Use indentations, moving across the page from left to right for main headings to subheadings and so on. Their location on the page will help you when you come to revise.

→ Make quotations from a book or article obvious, perhaps by highlighting them.

The difference between...

Good notes	**Why did Henry VIII want a divorce from Catherine of Aragon?**

	1. Need a male heir
	
	↓
	
	  • H concerned about succession — could Mary succeed?
	  • C of A last pregnancy 1518
	
	    ↓
	
	    • Too old now to conceive
	    • Miscarriages/stillborn babies
	    • No longer sleeping with Henry
	  • Promoted illegitimate son, Henry Fitzroy
	
	2. Marriage against God's will
	
	  ↓
	
	  • Explains why no male child
	  • Fr ambassador qns. legit. of M
	  • Leviticus
	  • Growing concern for H
	  • Need legit. marriage
	
	    ↓
	
	    • Vital for T dynasty — legit. heir

Poor notes	The reasons for Henry VIII's divorce from Catherine of Aragon There are many reasons why Henry divorced Catherine. 1. His relationship with Catherine had been deteriorating over a number of years. He had stopped sleeping with her in 1524. Catherine was, by 1524, aged 39 and had had several miscarriages and two stillborn babies. This meant that there was little chance of her having a male heir — last pregnancy was in 1518. 2. Henry needed to find a wife to provide him with a male heir. It was a concern — seen in the promotion of his illegitimate son Henry Fitzroy to be Duke of Richmond. 3. Henry fell in love with Anne Boleyn. Initially he wanted her to be his mistress and had no plans to marry her. However she refused to be just his mistress. Only in 1527 did Henry agree to marry Anne once he had obtained an annulment for his marriage to Catherine.

- The good notes are actual notes, not full sentences or prose.
- The good notes use abbreviations.
- The good notes are clearly laid out, using arrows and bullets to make separate points clear. There are no arrows or bullets in the poor notes.
- The good notes are stepped from left to right, with a lot of white space on the paper. With the poor notes the writing is more continuous — a page of notes like this would consist of solid text like a book.
- The key points that might form the basis of a paragraph are clearly identifiable in the good notes. The bullets provide the evidence that supports the main point being made.

Ensure that you keep your notes organised. Not only will this help you when you are writing essays, but it will also mean that when you start revising they are in the correct and logical order. You may find it helpful to buy a set of dividers or even better to design your own on which you can also write the contents of that section and link it to the exam board specification. This will be a useful check to ensure that your notes cover every part of the specification.

Similarly, if you are doing your notes on a computer, ensure that your files are organised and backed up. It might be helpful to have a folder for each key topic or issue in the specification, and again it might be helpful to create a summary page which tells you what is in that folder.

You should know

> **Think about why you are reading something before you begin.**
> **Remember there is a range of different reading techniques, all of which you will need to develop and practise.**
> **Always read with a purpose; passive reading is of little benefit.**
> **Make an effort to develop your own note-taking style.**
> **Do not copy out large amounts of text when taking notes.**
> **Do not note the same thing twice or try to write everything down in a lesson or lecture.**
> **Remember that you will need to read and take notes beyond the basic texts if you want to reach the highest levels.**

3 Writing a long essay

Learning objectives

> To be able to deconstruct an examination question so that you understand exactly what is being asked

> To understand what makes an effective introduction and conclusion

> To understand the importance of opening sentences for each paragraph

> To know how to structure a paragraph in a long-answer essay

> To be able to maintain a consistent line of argument throughout an essay

> To understand the difference between explaining and evaluating factors or issues

> To understand how to support ideas with precise and relevant factual material

Long essays form part of every examination paper you will take. Mastering the skill of essay-writing is therefore crucial if you are to achieve a high overall grade. This chapter will give you some general guidelines and advice to follow, but remember there is no single right way to write an essay.

There is also no shortcut to learning how to write a good essay. Although mark schemes may state that no set answer is required, there are still some rules that you should follow. It is worth looking again at assessment objective 1 (AO1; p. 14) as this makes clear the skills that you will need to do well:

→ analysis

→ evaluation

→ substantiated judgements

In other words, just learning facts and describing events will not get you very far — you have to master these higher-level skills. Although the types of question set by the different examination boards may vary, none of them will ask you to just 'describe' or 'explain' an event.

It is also worth checking what percentage of the final mark AO1 is worth as this will help you to realise its importance (see the Exam board focus section for the particular examination board you are following).

Deconstructing the question

Unless you understand what a question is asking, you will not be able to answer it effectively. However, many students give the impression, in the way they approach an essay, that they have not

> **! Common pitfall**
>
> Sometimes candidates have written an essay on a similar topic before and learnt it for the exam. When a slightly different question comes up, they simply regurgitate it without paying attention to any slightly different words, phrases or emphasis. When candidates adopt this approach they are very unlikely to score well.

read the question carefully and thought about how to answer it. They appear to simply see the question and rush into writing an answer without stopping to work out what they are actually being asked to do.

You are never asked to simply write all you know about an event, issue or person — it is not a memory test. Rather you are being tested on your ability to *use* what you know to answer a specific question. It is therefore important that you can see the difference between answering the actual question set and writing all you know about a topic.

The difference between...

Assess the reasons why Henry VIII broke from Rome.

Answering the question set	Writing everything I know
• The need for a male heir • Catherine's inability to produce a male heir • Love for Anne Boleyn • Concerns about the validity of the dispensation • To gain power and money • Unable to obtain an annulment	• Henry had stopped sleeping with Catherine • Catherine's age • Foreign situation • Wolsey's failure to get a divorce from the pope despite promises • Importance of the Boleyn faction • Condition of the church in England • Promotion of the Duke of Richmond • Henry's trip to France • The legislation passed by Parliament • Anti-clerical feeling in Parliament • Love letters to Anne • Catherine's attitude

The material in the right-hand column might be accurate but is not always relevant to the question set. The question is not about what happened — it is about why it happened and involves more than just Henry's divorce from Catherine of Aragon.

It is important that you develop the skill of deconstructing long-answer questions. You will need to look for a number of elements (perhaps devising a mnemonic based on 'CTFL' to remind yourself):

→ C: the **command words**

→ T: the **topic** of the question

→ F: the **focus** of the question

→ L: possible **limitations** to the question (these may not always be present)

We will look at each of these elements in turn.

Command words

The command words tell you what to do. In your essays these are most likely to be 'assess', 'to what extent', and 'how far' or 'how successful'. Table 3.1 explains what is required for each of these.

Table 3.1 Command words

Command words	What you need to do
Assess	Explain the relative importance of a list of factors in causing an event or the consequences of an event. Do not just explain a list of reasons as that will be little more than an unstructured list.
To what extent	You are being asked to make a judgement about 'extent'. It may be helpful to think in terms of a sliding scale. You will need to consider all of the evidence and not just the evidence for the named issue or factor before reaching a judgement as to where on the sliding scale the factor or answer should be. Not at all — Somewhat — Completely — Hardly — Mostly
How far	This is similar to the 'To what extent' question and the same advice applies to both. If you are asked about the importance of a factor or issue, it is vital to consider other factors as well. Don't ignore the named factor but don't write only about the named factor.
How successful	This question requires you to establish some criteria against which you can judge success. They might be themes such as economic and political, or they might be long and short term. You will need to reach a judgement for each issue and then an overall judgement based on the series of interim judgements.

Table 3.1 should have made it clear that you need to go beyond just explaining how something happened. You need to reach a judgement about the importance of the factors that brought about the event. This is the substantiated judgement that is part of AO1.

The topic

The topic tells you what area from the specification the question is on. It may refer to an event, a person or a policy — for example the October Revolution in Russia, Henry VIII or Nazi economic policy. Provided you have covered and revised all of the elements in the specification that make up your study area or key topics, then these should come as no surprise.

In some instances the topic may be quite broad, as in Elizabeth I's religious policy, while in others it may be quite narrow, as in the Dissolution of the Monasteries.

However, it is not enough just to identify the topic — you need to look carefully at the specific focus. For example, the topic may be Henry VIII's religious policy, but what is the focus within this? Does the question require you to write about his whole reign or just part of it? Simply rushing in could result in you wasting a lot of time and writing about material which does not answer the question, which will not score you any marks.

Focus

Once you have identified the topic, remember it is the specific focus that is crucial. There may be a number of words or phrases that make up the focus. These words or phrases will tell you which part of the topic you have to write about and, crucially, what the focus of your argument or debate should be.

> **! Common pitfall**
>
> Questions that ask 'How far' or 'To what extent' are not 'yes' or 'no' questions. You need to consider your level of agreement with the statement you have been given, and explain why you have reached that judgement.

> **! Common pitfall**
>
> Although the topic provides you with the broad focus of the question, it is not specific. One of the most common mistakes that candidates make is to identify the topic and then write all they know about that, without paying careful attention to the specific focus of the topic.

Annotated examples: essay questions

The example questions below are highlighted to illustrate their distinct elements.

Question 1

How successful was Wolsey's domestic policy?

Question 2

'Terror was the most important reason why Stalin was able to control the Russian people.' How far do you agree?

| The topic of the question | The focus of the question | The argument you should be writing about |

Activity

Can you identify the topic, the focus and the argument you should be writing about in these questions?

- How successful was the foreign policy of Henry VII?
- To what extent was England Protestant by the death of Henry VIII in 1547?
- How effectively did Elizabeth manage Parliament?
- 'Propaganda was the most important factor in the rise of support for Nazism.' How far do you agree?
- 'The most important reason why Adenauer was able to remain in power for so long was the economic miracle.' How far do you agree?
- How stable was Russia in the years from 1891 to 1914?
- How important was Trotsky in securing victory for the Bolsheviks in the Russian Civil War?

Limitations

Not all questions will have limitations, but you do need to be aware of them just in case they do. A limitation is a phrase or word in the question which limits what you can write about. In some instances this is very obvious — for example, it might be the time period you can discuss or an area of policy. If a question asks about domestic policy or events before the outbreak of the Second World War, then writing about foreign policy or events after 1939 will score very few, if any, marks.

However, there are occasions when the limitations are less obvious. There are sometimes small or unnoticed words that give context to the question that has been set. These are words such as 'increasingly' or 'less'. They suggest that there has been change over time which has made the debate more or less important. If you want to gain top marks then it is vital that you recognise these words and tailor your answer accordingly.

Such words may change a simple question on the success or failure of a policy into something more complex that requires you to focus specifically on a particular development. For example, there is a significant difference between these two questions:

→ 'Henry VII's foreign policy was not successful.' How far do you agree?

→ 'Henry VII's foreign policy became less successful towards the end of his reign.' How far do you agree?

or these:

→ 'Nazi economic policy failed to prepare Germany for war in 1939.' How far do you agree?

→ 'Nazi economic policy completely failed to prepare Germany for war in 1939.' How far do you agree?

The difference between...

A question with a limitation	A question without a limitation
'Stalin's rule of Russia was merely brutal and destructive.' How far do you agree?	**'Stalin's rule of Russia was brutal and destructive.' How far do you agree?**
Although there were elements that it could be argued were merely brutal and destructive, for example his policy towards the kulaks or the use of terror, it could also be argued that his rule of Russia was not merely brutal and destructive as: • the economy was modernised • Russia was able to win the Great Patriotic War • he turned Russia into a superpower	Although you may agree to a large extent that overall it was brutal and destructive, you could discuss each element of policy and decide 'how far'. Even if you noted that he modernised the economy, you would be likely to point out at what cost — and the same might apply to victory in the Great Patriotic War or turning Russia into a superpower.

Planning your answer

Once you have deconstructed the question you should be clear about what is actually required. However, it is now important to take some time to plan your answer.

Your plan is meant to provide you with the structure that your essay will follow. It should set out a clear line of argument. It should include the points you intend to cover in your answer and some of the examples you intend to use to support your argument. Finally it should state the conclusion or judgement you intend to reach.

Some of this may seem surprising, particularly knowing your conclusion before you start to write. However, if you think about it this is vital. It will ensure that you develop a consistent argument and do not change your view during the essay. This is why thinking and planning are so important: they allow you to consider a number of possible arguments and decide which is the most convincing before you start to write, rather than making up your mind as you write.

Knowing what you are going to conclude will also allow you to signpost to the examiner throughout the essay your line of argument so that by the time the examiner reaches the conclusion it will come as no surprise.

> **! Common pitfall**
>
> The pressure of time in the examination room results in large numbers of candidates rushing straight into writing. Planning is vital if you are to remain focused on the actual question set.

> **! Common pitfall**
>
> Avoid making a plan which simply lists dates or events to include in your answer. That kind of plan is likely to lead to a chronological and descriptive response rather than an analytical one which can reach the higher levels.

Annotated example: essay plan

Assess the reasons for the growth in support for the Nazi party in the period from 1924 to 1933.

Opening paragraph: range of reasons — including Hitler, weakness/inability of Weimar to deal with problems — but support really grows with rising unemployment in Depression, which suggests it is the most important reason.

Use of the word 'suggests' sets out the line of argument likely to be followed.

1. Rise in unemployment — Nazi support grows with rising unemployment, had not done well 1924–9 when lower unemployment. Nazis offer solution, appeals to those who lost jobs and paramilitary gives sense of belonging. Seats in Reichstag vs unemployment. Most important reason.

The importance of this factor is explained, with a list of reasons why it is important (rather than just a list of facts). A clear argument is shown with this as the most important reason.

2. Failure of the Republic — government unable to agree policy on unemployment benefit so appears weak, encourages people to look for alternatives — link to 1.

Explanation, but also a link is shown which will be developed/explained in the essay.

3. Leadership of Hitler — appeal, image and ability as orator, portrayed as the superman to solve problems and restore pride. Compare with Weimar politicians. Hitler at centre of propaganda. Link to 2.

Explanation and further awareness of link.

4. Reorganisation of Nazi party — recovery 1923–4 allows Nazis to take advantage of 1 and 2, use Hitler's abilities in 3. Local leaders well trained and disciplined.

Links between factors are further developed.

5. Fear of communism — fear Germany develop as USSR, Nazis play on this, disrupt communist meetings and then restore order claiming only party who could. Win support of businessmen and middle class who fear communism.

No real link can be developed from this to Weimar's failure to deal with this threat.

> 6. Conclusion — link between factors, but unemployment crucial and exploited by Nazis who claim Weimar too weak to deal with it, central message of propaganda (last hope) and speeches. ◀

Links which have been shown in the main body are stressed and there is some explanation.

The plan gives a clear structure. The links between the factors follow logically and this will help with the flow of the essay (for more on flow, see p. 38). The line of argument is consistent. There is not a long list of facts — instead the plan shows how material will be used to pursue an argument.

Writing the opening paragraph

One of the most common pitfalls in essay writing is spending a long time writing an introduction that will gain very few or even no marks. Often there is little important content — just like an 'introduction' between two strangers who spend the first few minutes exchanging pleasantries with little of substance being said. Perhaps worse, a student may simply rewrite the question in their own words, or copy it out and then add 'and this will be the focus of my answer'.

It is important to construct an effective opening paragraph. Very few students are taught how to do this, but it is quite easy if you follow some pointers.

In your opening paragraph you should:
→ Give your view about the issue in the question — state your opinion, or hint at what you are likely to argue and why.
→ Identify the issues or factors you intend to discuss and show how they link to the question.
→ Show your awareness of the debate the question raises.

Annotated example: essay introduction

Assess the reasons why the Nazi party was so concerned about the education of young people in Germany.

> There were many reasons why the Nazi party was so concerned about education in Germany. These reasons were linked to the future of Germany and the indoctrination of the young, as well as the roles that they had to play. It is important to

consider the role that they would have to play in the future and why therefore the Nazis were so concerned about education. All of these factors help to explain why they were so concerned.

This is not a strong introduction. It does show that the student is aware that there were a number of reasons why the Nazi party was concerned, but provided the student has turned up to lessons and done some revision that should be expected! Although the answer suggests that there were a number of reasons, it does not offer a view about the importance of those reasons. The introduction could also be much clearer in identifying the reasons and showing how they will be developed in the following paragraphs. That might seem quite a lot to write, but it is not really.

You should now be able to see why a good opening paragraph is vital. It provides the examiner with a clear signpost as to the direction your answer will take and the issues you intend to cover. This means that, provided you stick to it, the direction of your essay will not come as a surprise. The last thing an examiner wants is to be taken on a mystery tour, discovering only at the very end what your view is. So set out your view in your opening paragraph and then structure your answer to support that view and show the examiner why it is the best explanation and why others have greater limitations.

Activity

Using the information from this and the previous sections, write an opening paragraph to at least one of the essay questions below, ensuring that you keep fully focused on the question.

- How much opposition was there to Henry VIII's religious policies?
- Assess the reasons for Elizabeth I's financial problems.
- 'Hitler was only ever a weak dictator.' How far do you agree?
- How successful were the years 1924–9 for the Weimar Republic?
- 'Stalin's economic policies were a disaster for Russia.' How far do you agree?
- 'Russia's performance in the First World War was the main reason for the fall of the tsar.' How far do you agree?

Writing an analytical and evaluative essay

Once you have written that vital opening paragraph, you are on to writing the main body of the essay. The essay needs to be persuasive. It might help to imagine that you are a lawyer presenting a case for the prosecution where you need to show not just why your view is correct but also why other views are wrong — you can't simply ignore or dismiss other opinions. There is no set way to do this and if you try and devise a formula you will lose the spontaneity and passion that are needed to write a good answer.

What to avoid

The most common errors are either to write a descriptive answer or to tell the examiner everything about the topic, some of which will not be relevant. Deconstructing the question and drawing up a structured plan should help you to avoid irrelevance, but you also need to take care to avoid the descriptive answer which includes relevant knowledge but does not use it to answer the actual question. Sometimes the argument may be implicit (i.e. suggested by the material but not directly expressed), but then the examiner is having to work to see how the material is linked to the question.

Annotated example: essay paragraph

How important was Wolsey's lack of noble support in bringing about his fall from power?

The paragraph is about a factor that is relevant to the question set. However, the paragraph does not explain how it led to his fall.

The answer simply describes the events of 1525 from Pavia through to the rebellion and its defeat.

The Amicable Grant rebellion was another cause of Wolsey's fall. Charles had defeated the French king at the Battle of Pavia in 1525 and as a result Henry wanted to invade France and claim the French throne. However, there was no money available for the invasion and therefore Wolsey attempted to raise money without calling Parliament. The clergy and laity were expected to pay this, but earlier 'loans' had not been repaid and therefore there was opposition and resistance to the new tax. This opposition developed into rebellion in East Anglia and the Dukes of Norfolk and Suffolk had to put down the unrest. When Henry heard of the unrest he claimed that he did not know about the raising of the grant and blamed Wolsey. Wolsey took the blame and this helped bring about his fall.

There is some implied argument that the new tax caused opposition and that this helped in his downfall.

There is an assertion that this helped to bring about his fall, but the paragraph has not really shown how.

Structuring an essay

Each paragraph should discuss a point or issue relevant to the question. It should be obvious, even from the opening sentence of the paragraph, how the idea or issue you are going to discuss relates to the actual question set.

This has important implications for the first sentence of each paragraph. It is really beneficial if that sentence introduces an idea that relates directly to the question and you then go on in the rest of the paragraph to discuss that idea before making an interim judgement about it in relation to the question.

This will mean that the last sentence of each paragraph also links back directly to the question, ensuring that you have not lost sight of it and that you have made the examiner aware of how you are developing your argument.

In practice, this means that each paragraph is rather like a mini essay:

→ The opening sentence introduces the idea to be discussed.

→ The main body of the paragraph discusses the idea in a balanced way.

→ The last sentence reaches a judgement about the issue discussed in relation to the question.

Your plan will have identified the issues that you are going to discuss in the essay. Now, for each one of those ideas, you need an opening sentence that links the idea to the question being discussed.

Consider the following question:

Assess the reasons why Hitler was appointed chancellor in January 1933.

Now look at the following possible opening sentences for paragraphs within the essay:

→ The Depression played a crucial role in gaining Hitler support as it exposed the weaknesses in the Weimar system of government and encouraged people to look for alternatives.

→ The personal impact that Hitler had on the people ensured that they looked to him rather than other alternatives, particularly the communists.

→ Hitler provided the German people with scapegoats for their problems and argued that only he could deal with them.

→ The organisation of the Nazi party, particularly with its propaganda, ensured it won popular support.

→ However, what finally brought Hitler to power was not electoral success but intrigue within the political system.

By reading just these opening sentences you gain a clear idea of the issues that the student will discuss, and also of what they consider to be important reasons and which they consider to be the most important. It might come as a surprise that not one of the sentences is simply a factual statement — instead each sentence offers a view about an issue that relates to the question.

Activity

Consider the following question:

How successful was Adenauer as chancellor of West Germany in the period 1949–63?

Look at the following possible opening sentences for paragraphs. Which ones introduce an idea relevant to the question and which are simply factual statements?

- Adenauer ensured that democracy was established and presided over a period of political stability which was in stark contrast to Weimar.

- Adenauer won an overall majority in the 1957 election.

➡

- Electoral triumphs throughout the period suggest that his chancellorship was a success.
- In many ways, the economic performance of West Germany during this period was the most successful aspect of his premiership.
- Marshall Aid brought in only $2 billion by October 1954.
- In 1953 Adenauer ignored the Berlin uprising.
- Adenauer was less successful in his dealings with the Soviet Union.
- His handling of the construction of the Berlin Wall was less than successful.
- Adenauer was able to successfully integrate West Germany with the rest of western Europe.
- West Germany joined the EEC, OEEC and NATO.

Activity

Now write six paragraph-opening sentences for at least one of the following essay questions:

- How successful was the reign of Mary Tudor?
- How serious a threat to Elizabeth I was Mary Stuart, Queen of Scots?
- 'The Depression was the most important reason for the failure of the Weimar Republic.' How far do you agree?
- Assess the reasons why Germany was divided in 1949.
- Assess the reasons why there were two revolutions in Russia in 1917.
- How far were Stalin's political skills responsible for his rise to power by 1928?

Discussing the ideas

You will need to discuss both sides of each idea you have introduced and decide which argument or interpretation is more convincing and why. Do not ignore the other side of the argument. If you do then you are unlikely to be able to explain why one side is more persuasive than the other. It may even suggest that you are not aware that there are two sides to the argument.

However, once you have considered both sides of the argument it is vital that you reach a supported judgement about which is the more convincing. You need to explain why it is more convincing, as otherwise it is just an assertion and will not score many marks. Recall that AO1 mentions 'making substantiated judgements'. If there are judgements about each issue you have discussed and also an overall judgement (which will be considered when we look at conclusions), then you will have satisfied that part of the assessment objective.

> **! Common pitfall**
>
> Do not ignore one side of the argument. Ensure that you discuss both sides before reaching a judgement about the issue.

Annotated example: longer essay paragraph

How successful were Elizabeth I and her ministers in managing Parliament?

This is a longer example of a paragraph, but it illustrates many of the points that have been stressed above.

The number of powers available to Elizabeth in order to manage Parliament ensured that she was mostly successful. She possessed the ultimate weapon in that through her prerogative she had the power to summon, prorogue, adjourn and dissolve Parliament. Elizabeth was therefore able to call them when she wanted and this was done only rarely, usually when she needed money, as in the 1590s to finance war. As she was able to obtain considerable sums from them, even during a period of rapid inflation and increasing financial pressure, it was evident that she was successful in achieving her goal. However, it was not just her powers that meant she was successful, as she was also helped by the fact that most MPs did not want to stay in London for too long as it was expensive. As a result, some did not attend and many who did were more concerned about local issues than national ones and therefore were not difficult to manage. On many occasions, once taxes had been granted Elizabeth saw little need to prolong the session and many MPs were more than happy to return home, suggesting that the meetings were not difficult to manage. This is made even clearer by the lack of MPs who spoke in debates and the numbers who actually bothered to vote, suggesting that most matters were not controversial and therefore there was little difficulty in managing an institution that was largely subservient.

The opening sentence introduces an idea directly related to the question.

Support for the argument is provided and explained in relation to the question.

The argument is balanced as it explains that it was not just Elizabeth's powers that allowed her to manage Parliament.

A judgement about the issue discussed is reached, suggesting that it was Parliament's subservience rather than Elizabeth's powers that made management easy.

Once you have written a strong paragraph, it is important to ensure that this fits into the overall structure of your essay. Remember that your job is to convince the examiner of your view. It is not your job to outline all the possible arguments but to persuade the person reading your essay that your view is right. To do this, you need a clear structure to your line of argument.

> ✓ **Exam tip**
>
> Remember that the examiner will be aware of the knowledge you use — what he or she won't know is your view. The examiner will want to be convinced that it is right, or at least can stand up to analysis, so you need to write persuasively.

The difference between...

How far were the Western powers to blame for the division of Germany in 1949?

A strong persuasive structure	A weak persuasive structure
Introduction	Introduction
Most significant point that they were to blame • including discussion of for and against • line of argument FOR	Most significant point FOR
	Most significant point AGAINST
Point • including for and against in one paragraph • line of argument FOR	Point 2 FOR
	Point 2 AGAINST
Point • including for and against in one paragraph • line of argument AGAINST	Point 3 FOR
	Point 3 AGAINST
Least significant point • including for and against in one paragraph • line of argument FOR	Point 4 FOR
	Point 4 AGAINST
Conclusion	Conclusion
Comment: In this essay the student has written fewer paragraphs, but in each paragraph both sides of a point are discussed and a judgement is reached. They have not included any fewer arguments that it was not the West who was to blame than the other approach, but within each paragraph they have shown why the argument that the West was to blame outweighs the view that the USSR was to blame in most instances. This approach is much more likely to remain focused on the question and reach a judgement based on the line of argument in the essay.	*Comment: While this student shows that they have a lot of knowledge, they have produced a totally balanced essay which suggests that the arguments for and against are equal. This suggests that their analysis and evaluation of the issues will be weaker. This approach is more likely to rely on telling the examiner everything the student knows, rather than producing a convincing argument with a judgement that is supported by the essay.*

The flow

If you look back at the section on planning (p. 30) or even the example above, it is clear that each paragraph should consider a different point. However, your essay also needs to flow from one point to the next. Here links between points are particularly helpful, but you can also use words and phrases that help to link the paragraphs together. Then, although each paragraph is a self-contained discussion, it will lead to the next point and the argument will be continually developed. You could use words and phrases such as:

→ 'While...'
→ 'Despite this...'
→ 'Moreover...'
→ 'Although...'
→ 'However...'
→ 'In addition...'
→ 'It is also important...'
→ 'On the other hand...'

Look again at the example above on the division of Germany. Here you could link paragraphs together in the following way. The third paragraph might open like this, following from the argument that the West was most to blame:

→ Despite this, the decisions made by both sides at the end of the war meant that cooperation was unlikely.

The fourth paragraph might then open as follows:

→ However, in the short term it does appear as if the West must take most of the responsibility as it was they who began the process of currency reform knowing that the USSR would oppose it.

This type of approach is important as it helps to make your essay read like a continuous and persuasive piece of writing.

Writing a conclusion

Much like the vital opening paragraph, the conclusion can cause serious problems for students. Many do not know how to write a conclusion properly and sometimes, in an examination, students simply run out of time. In some answers a conclusion might consist of just one sentence that adds nothing to the essay. Yet a good conclusion is vital if you are to reach the top level.

Why are conclusions important?

Although you should be making a series of interim judgements about each issue or factor throughout the essay, the conclusion is your opportunity to pull those together and provide an overall judgement. As mentioned earlier, AO1 requires you to make substantiated judgements, and the conclusion is where this should be done. It is a requirement of all the examination boards if you want to get the top marks.

Consider again some of the command words or phrases:

→ 'To what extent...'
→ 'How far...'

The conclusion is your opportunity to explain the 'extent' or 'how far'. Answers to these kinds of questions are not just 'yes' or 'no'. In the essay you will have considered a range of issues relating to the question, but now you need to take an overall view based on the sum of those issues. The conclusion will therefore give a direct answer to the question.

It might be helpful to think about it in the following way:

→ In the vital opening paragraph you set out what you thought might be the answer, using words like 'suggest'.

→ In the main body of the essay you considered both sides of the argument and reached a series of interim judgements about each issue.

→ In the conclusion you bring all that together and can now confirm your initial view — based on all the issues, factors or themes you have discussed — and briefly explain why. You are acting here like a judge giving your verdict based on the evidence in the main body of your essay.

> **! Common pitfall**
>
> A conclusion should come to a judgement based on what you have already written. It should not introduce new ideas — if they were important they should have been discussed in the main body of the essay.

> **! Common pitfall**
>
> In the conclusion, take care to avoid offering a contrary argument to the one you have pursued throughout the rest of the essay. That would suggest to the examiner that you have not thought through your ideas and are unclear about what you really think.

> **✓ Exam tip**
>
> Ensure that you support your conclusion with some evidence. Otherwise it is just an assertion, not a judgement.

Annotated example: conclusion

'Henry VIII's foreign policy in the 1540s was a failure.' How far do you agree?

This shows that even though he appears to achieve his aims this needs to be qualified, so the judgement is balanced.

Once again the judgement shows balance and the response goes on to support the counter view.

Henry's foreign policy in the 1540s went a long way to achieving his aims; he had carried out his obligation as a monarch to wage war and had brought the nation glory on the battlefield at Solway Moss and in capturing Boulogne, even though the prestige was often short-lived. However, this must be balanced against the cost for the nation, with over £2 million spent on war in the last decade. His policy towards Scotland had created deeper hostility and failed to achieve his ultimate aim of unity, while the gains in France were short-term and costly. However, against these costs Henry had been able to protect national security which was the most important consideration and by bringing prestige and glory he had fulfilled his aims, but at the expense of a financial problem that would last for many years.

The opening sentence does appear to offer an overall judgement.

An overall judgement is reached, but it is balanced: Henry achieved his aims and protected the nation but at a cost. The judgement is therefore one of a qualified success.

Activity

Write a conclusion to at least one of the following questions:
- 'The church in England on the eve of the Reformation was in need of urgent reform.' To what extent do you agree?
- 'Support for Elizabeth I declined in the period after 1588.' How far do you agree?
- How serious were the threats to the Weimar Republic in the period from 1919 to 1923?
- How much opposition was there to Nazi rule?
- Assess the reasons why the Provisional Government was short-lived.
- 'White weaknesses were the most important reason for Bolshevik success in the Civil War.' How far do you agree?

How to develop your essay-writing skills

You must not forget that you are working towards the final examination after either 1 or 2 years and it is what you achieve in that examination that really matters. Everything you do should be seen as a step along that path and a step towards reaching that ultimate goal. However, unless you are fortunate you will find that there are times when your essays do not seem to improve. Do not be surprised as this is quite normal, and after a while you should see an improvement. There are things you can do to help yourself continue to develop even if this is not initially reflected in your essays:

→ Do not panic.

→ Continue to do what you have been doing well.

→ Look at the comments at the end of each marked essay.

→ Act on the advice at the end of each marked essay — this is more important than the mark you have achieved.

→ Reread your essays and highlight in different colours things that you did well and things you could improve.

→ Ensure that you repeat the things you did well in the next essay.

→ Avoid the things that were less successful.

Reviewing your essays

Self-evaluation is a great skill to develop and you will find it particularly helpful when you come to do your coursework.

Take it further

Conduct a SWOT analysis of one of your essays, using the checklists below to help you:

● Strengths — what areas worked particularly well and why?

● Weaknesses — what areas were weak and how can you improve them?

● Opportunities — what additional steps can you take to improve your writing?

● Threats — what areas do you find particularly difficult and how can you overcome these difficulties?

The mark scheme for your examination board should help you identify the skills you need to display. Go through each essay paragraph by paragraph and check the following points:

→ Is there focus on the question in each paragraph?

→ Does the opening sentence introduce an idea that relates to the question?

→ Is there an argument?

→ Is the argument strong or weak?

→ Is the argument supported by relevant and accurate knowledge?

→ Is the argument balanced? Have both sides of the argument been considered?

→ Are there interim judgements?

→ Is there an overall judgement?

→ Is the judgement supported?

→ Does the judgement follow from the main body of the essay?

This checklist will allow you to identify areas where you are doing well and where you need to maintain that level and areas where you need to develop.

It is also helpful to consider where on a scale — from excellent, very good, good, satisfactory to weak — you would place the following elements of each essay:

→ focus on the question
→ opening paragraph
→ argument
→ supporting knowledge for the argument
→ interim judgements
→ overall judgement

Using the two checklists for reviewing your essays given above (the list of questions and the list of elements to be rated on a scale), set yourself targets for the areas to improve in your next piece of work, while maintaining the same level in the other areas. It is worth remembering that you cannot improve everything at once. Instead you will improve gradually and through practice. If you look back after a term at the earlier essays you wrote, you will notice how far you have improved.

Improving your writing skills

There are a number of other ways you can improve your writing skills. It is worth going back to Chapter 2, on reading and note-taking, and refreshing your memory about reading skills. When you read, look at how authors structure their arguments, how they use their evidence to support their claims and how they discuss issues.

It is also worth swapping essays with your friends. You can then see how they have approached the same question. You might notice how they use opening sentences or make links between paragraphs.

Once you have done all this, it is sometimes worthwhile to rewrite part of an essay that you have done, taking on board all you have learnt from following the above suggestions. Your teacher will be more than happy to look at this; if you are willing to put in the extra time to improve, they will be impressed and support you. The key is not to be disheartened if your writing takes time to improve and not to forget the end goal.

You should know

> **Deconstruct the essay question so that you remain focused on the question and answer what has been set.**

> **Plan your essay so that it focuses on the question and is not just a list of everything you know.**

> **Write an opening paragraph which briefly outlines your argument and the issues you will discuss.**

> **Ensure that your essay has a consistent line of argument.**

> **Ensure that you write an effective conclusion that focuses on the overall line of argument of your essay and not each individual issue.**

> **Use feedback from essays, redraft parts of your work and read other responses to help develop your essay style.**

4 Working with sources

Learning objectives

> To be able to identify the view of the source you are studying
> To be able to consider the provenance of a source when analysing primary sources
> To use contextual knowledge to evaluate primary and secondary sources
> To use evaluative words and develop an evaluative vocabulary in order to evaluate sources

In your A-level history course you will encounter two different types of sources: primary and secondary. Primary sources are written at the time of the event or very close to its occurrence, while secondary sources are written much later and are likely to have been written by historians or commentators. The skills you need to handle these do have points in common, but there are also some differences you should keep in mind, particularly when dealing with secondary sources or interpretations.

You should be aware that all examination boards require you to analyse primary and secondary sources or different interpretations, as made clear by assessment objectives 2 and 3. Analysis of sources is examined in a number of ways, but all examination boards require you to analyse at least primary sources in an exam. You will also find this chapter helpful when you are doing your coursework, as examination boards require you to use primary or secondary sources and sometimes both in your essay.

Reading a source

It is likely that during your course you will read a considerable number of primary sources, but as with your other reading, you need to ask yourself why you are reading the source. It is very unlikely that any exam question will simply require you to paraphrase or summarise a source. Although you might think of this as your first step, it certainly cannot be the end of the process.

Even to summarise a source, you will need to have an understanding of the period you are studying and the key developments that were taking place. You will also need to be aware of any particular terminology or concepts which are associated with that period and often referred to by contemporary writers. If you are studying the Tudor period, for example, and are looking at the social and economic problems of the mid-Tudor period, it would be helpful to know that many writers explained the problems in moral terms.

It is probably helpful then to adopt a three-strand approach to dealing with a source:

→ Read the source and ensure you understand what it is saying.

→ Read the source more closely and work out what its view is about the issue you are studying.

→ Find evidence in the source to support the view.

It might be useful to have a highlighter available when you are working with a source or a group of sources. Then, when you come to the final part of the process, where you are identifying evidence in the source that supports the view, you can highlight it. It might be even better to have two different-coloured highlighters so that you can use contrasting colours to highlight evidence that supports or challenges the view of the question or issue you are studying.

If you studied history at GCSE, you probably found that it was usually quite straightforward to identify evidence that supported or challenged a view. However, at AS and A-level it may be less obvious so you will need to look for inferences.

> **! Common pitfall**
>
> When reading sources, candidates often just look at what the source says in general terms — instead it is important to focus on what it says about the issue in either the question or the topic being studied.

Activity

Read Source 1, which describes the restoration of Catholicism in 1553–4, and then consider the questions which follow.

Source 1

From August 1553 in many places in Yorkshire, priests were very glad to say mass in Latin, according to the fervent zeal and love they had unto God and his laws. Holy bread and water was given, altars were rebuilt, pictures and images set up once more. The English service was voluntarily laid aside and the Latin mass taken up again, and all without compulsion of any Act or law, but merely on the wish of Queen Mary. And all the old ceremonies were used regularly, once the Lord Cardinal Pole arrived in this realm in November 1554.

(Robert Parkyn, 'A Narrative of the Reformation')

Questions

● What view does the source express about the restoration of Catholicism?

● What evidence does the source provide in support of the view it expresses?

It might be helpful to think about the adjectives you would use to describe the view of the source you are analysing. For example, you might argue that Source 1 above is **passionate** in its support of the restoration of Catholicism. You should then think about what evidence there is in the source to support your description. For example, what evidence is there in Source 1 to show that the writer is passionate?

In thinking like this about how to describe the author's view, you will have started to interpret the evidence, but it is also important to link it to the issue in the question and decide what the evidence is saying about that issue. Try to apply this approach when reading Source 2 in the activity below.

The importance of provenance

Activity

Consider the source below and decide what it is saying about why people supported Lady Jane Grey: was it because of religion or were other factors more important in determining whether people supported her or Mary?

Source 2

After King Edward's death the Council proclaimed Lady Jane as queen. But, partly because of the right of Mary's title and partly because of the malice that the people bore to the Duke of Northumberland for the death of the Duke of Somerset and his other cruelty, the majority of the commons with some nobles sided with Lady Mary, who proclaimed herself queen.

It can be helpful to construct a table like Table 4.1 below, if you are dealing with a group of sources.

Table 4.1 Sources: views and evidence

Source	View of key issue	Evidence from the source
A		
B		
C		

Simply understanding what the source is saying about an issue and being able to explain it will not in itself score you high marks. However, unless you can do this you won't be able to go on to the next stages.

The importance of provenance

When analysing primary sources the issue of provenance is crucial. You will need to think about a number of points relating to provenance and analyse their impact on the validity of what the source is saying:

→ Who wrote the source?
→ When was the source written?
→ Why was the source written?
→ Is the view typical of the time?
→ What is the tone of the language used?

In discussing these points, it is no use just describing who wrote it, when it was written and so on — you need to explain how that could affect the validity of the view it is offering.

Who wrote the source?

In considering the origin of the source you will need to think about the role of the person at the time they wrote it and whether they would have been in a position to know about the events they are describing or whether they were relying on other accounts. You may also need to consider whether the author was a supporter or opponent of the government, regime or monarch they are commenting on. You may be aware that the person who wrote the

 Exam tip

In considering why a source was written you need to look at the nature of the source. If it is a private letter or a diary entry, it is likely to be recording the personal view of the author. If it is a letter from an ambassador to his ruler, it is likely to have been written to inform. However, if it is a speech or a government instruction it might inform, but it is also likely to be trying to persuade or to justify the view of the author.

 Exam tip

In order to address issues of provenance, it is vital that you read the rubric at the beginning and the attribution at the end of the source as they will often provide some of the information that you need.

Aiming for an A in A-level History

(45)

account had been rewarded or punished by the regime. It might also be helpful to consider the political or religious view of the author as this too can have an impact on their outlook.

Activity

Read this speech by Vyshinsky, the prosecutor at the third show trial in the USSR in March 1938, and consider the question below.

Source 3

Our country is awaiting and demanding one thing. The traitors and spies who were selling our country must be shot like dirty dogs! Our people are demanding one thing: crush the accursed reptile. Time will pass. The graves of the hateful traitors will grow over with weeds and thistles. But over us our sun will shine as bright and luminous as before. Along the road cleared of the last scum and filth of the past, we, with our beloved leaders and teacher, the great Stalin at our head, will march as before onwards and onwards towards communism.

Question

How would the fact that the speech is from the prosecutor affect the reliability of the source?

When was it written?

The date of the source can often be crucial as it will allow you to place it in the context of historical developments. This means that you need a very secure chronological understanding and timeline of the period you are studying. The time when a source is written can have a considerable impact on its view. Was the author writing just before or after a significant event, or perhaps some time after an event when they could analyse its longer-term impact?

Activity

Read these two sources and look carefully at when they were written. Think about the historical context and its likely influence on what was written, before reading the commentary below.

Source 4

However it has come to pass I cannot tell, but of late your Grace [Somerset] is grown in great choleric fashions, whenever you are challenged in that which you have conceived. A king who discourages men to give their opinions freely brings great hurt and peril to the realm. But a subject in great authority, as your Grace is, using such methods, is likely to fall in to great danger and peril.

(A letter from Sir William Paget to the Duke of Somerset, 8 May 1549)

Source 5

I told your grace the truth and was not believed. The king's subjects are out of all discipline, out of obedience, caring neither for protector nor king. And what is the cause? Your own softness, your intention to be good to the poor. Consider, I beg you most humbly, that society in a realm is maintained by means of religion and law. The use of the old religion is forbidden by a law, and the use of the new is not yet embraced by eleven out of twelve parts of the realm. As for the law, the foot takes on him part of the head, and the common people are behaving like a king.

➡

Remember what you promised me in the gallery at Westminster before the breath was out of the body of the king that is dead. Remember what you promised immediately after, devising with me concerning the place which you now occupy and that was to follow mine advice in all your proceedings more than any other man's. Which promise I wish your grace had kept.

(A letter from Sir William Paget to the Duke of Somerset, 7 July 1549)

Commentary

In the first letter Sir William Paget is warning Somerset that he should listen to advice and not just follow his own views. In the second letter to Somerset, written two months later, Paget is more forthright in his views. He attacks Somerset's methods and failure to listen to him.

Unless you were aware of the developments that had taken place in the two months between the letters, you would be unable to explain the change in attitude. By July 1549 unrest had broken out in much of southern and central England. The Western Rebellion had grown in size and was presenting a challenge to the government. However, Kett's rebellion was only just starting. Therefore, taking into account the date of the letter, we can work out that Paget's change in attitude would have been prompted by the troubles in the West Country rather than those in East Anglia, of which he was unlikely to be aware as the rebels were only just gathering.

Why was it written?

It is important to consider the purpose of the source. Was the source written to be published or was it a private letter or a diary? A document written for public consumption may express a different view to something written in a diary or in a private letter.

However, when commenting on the nature of the source be careful to avoid simplistic or generic comments about the source type. You need to explain why it might be more or less reliable. You should consider whether the author was trying to win support or persuade others to adopt a particular point of view. It is also worth thinking carefully about a source that appears to have been written to inform, such as a letter from an ambassador to his ruler: was it really written just to inform or would it still have a particular viewpoint?

Activity

Read the following source in which Goebbels gives his reaction to Kristallnacht, and answer the questions that follow.

Source 6

The justifiable and understandable indignation of the German people at the cowardly murder of a German diplomat in Paris was widely displayed last night. In numerous towns and villages of the Reich, reprisals were carried out against Jewish buildings and places of business. The whole population is now firmly asked to abstain from all further action of whatever nature against the Jews. The final reply to the Jewish outrage in Paris will be given to the Jews by legal means.

(A press statement issued by Joseph Goebbels about the events of Kristallnacht)

➡

Questions

- What had happened to Jewish people in Germany on Kristallnacht?
- What does Goebbels demand?
- Why might he demand this?
- Why might he say that the final reply will be given by legal means?
- What is he hoping to achieve by this statement?

Activity

Look again at the speech above by Vyshinsky (Source 3) and consider these questions:

- What is the purpose of his speech?
- How might that affect what he says?

Is the view typical?

The next point concerns whether the view expressed in the source is typical. This is probably the most complex of the issues you might need to consider. This could involve looking at where it was written: for example, would a Yorkshire priest in 1554 have the same view about religious developments as a priest from the south, and would they even know about developments in the south? You might need to consider whether the view is representative of people of a similar social class and, if not, whether that makes the view more or less reliable.

> ✅ **Exam tip**
>
> Ensure that you have identified the view of the whole passage and that you are not just focusing on one word or phrase in the interpretation or source.

Activity

Read the following source in which the officials of parish churches in the diocese of Canterbury, a centre of Protestantism, are ordered to fit out their churches for Catholic worship. To what extent do you think the situation indicated by this source would have been typical for the whole of England? Consider this issue before reading the commentary below.

Source 7

Goodnestone Church:

To provide front cloths for the altar for holy days, and a canopy and veil for Lent.

To make a new lock for the font.

The Chapel of Well, in Ickham

The Chapel is utterly decayed; the two bells are taken away, by whom it is certainly not known.

Goudhurst church:

To provide two decent banners before Rogation week. To repair the chancel ceiling, and the glass windows of the church.

(From Archdeacon Harpsfield's visitation of Canterbury Archdeaconry, 1557)

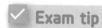

Commentary

These instructions were written just a year before Mary Tudor died and therefore it might be argued that churches still did not have the furnishings needed for Catholic services. However, this comes from the south of England where Protestantism was much stronger and the process of restoring Catholic ornaments would have been slower.

Were the problems encountered in Canterbury similar to those in other areas of England, particularly the north, where Catholicism was much stronger? How typical was Canterbury of the problems facing the Marian restoration? You would need knowledge of the regional differences to be able to explain whether the situation indicated by this source was typical of the whole of England or whether it was the exception, with the restoration being much easier in other areas.

What is the tone of the source?

In reading a source carefully, you may notice that some of the language used appears to be 'loaded' or exaggerated, either in a positive or a negative way. This can help you understand whether the author supports or opposes a particular point of view or person and can help you assess the validity of the view they are offering. Even official government documents may adopt a tone that is not neutral if their aim is to persuade.

Activity

Read the following source and identify any 'loaded' words or phrases that suggest the source might be unreliable in its analysis of the effectiveness of Nazi propaganda.

Source 8

We have witnessed many great march-pasts and ceremonies. But none of them was more thrilling, and at the same time more inspiring, than yesterday's roll call of 140,000 political wardens, who were addressed by the Führer at night, on the Zeppelin meadow which floodlights had made as bright as day. It is hardly possible to let words describe the mood and strength of this hour.

(Report from a local newspaper in 1936)

Activity

Look back at the speech by Vyshinsky at the show trial (Source 3) and identify any 'loaded' words and phrases. Why would he use such language?

You should have seen from the examples above that it is often impossible to separate the different elements of provenance. For example, the purpose and tone of the passages from both Goebbels and Vyshinsky are a clear indication that the source may not be completely reliable in its view.

! Common pitfall

Avoid comments such as 'It is from a diary and therefore will tell the truth' or 'It is a government act and is therefore reliable', which simply express generic assumptions about a source type. Instead you need to explain why a source might be more or less reliable.

Applying contextual knowledge

Contextual knowledge should be used to evaluate both primary and secondary sources or interpretations. However, the key word here is 'used'. Contextual knowledge should not simply be 'dumped' into your answer. A few well-chosen pieces of supporting material clearly linked to the source or interpretation are much more effective than lots of knowledge about the topic which is not well linked to the source or interpretation.

Whether it is a primary or secondary source you will be using contextual knowledge in exactly the same way. You may need to use some contextual knowledge to explain the content of the source or interpretation and place it in context, but this on its own will not score many marks. It is the next step that is important: using knowledge that either supports or challenges the view offered by the source or interpretation about the issue in the question.

Annotated example: responses to a source

Read the following source again (it is the same as Source 1 above), then compare the two responses below, considering how knowledge has been used to evaluate the view expressed in the source about support for the restoration of Catholicism in the period 1553–8.

Source 9

From August 1553 in many places in Yorkshire, priests were very glad to say mass in Latin, according to the fervent zeal and love they had unto God and his laws. Holy bread and water was given, altars were rebuilt, pictures and images set up once more. The English service was voluntarily laid aside and the Latin mass taken up again, and all without compulsion of any act or law, but merely on the wish of Queen Mary. And all the old ceremonies were used regularly, once the Lord Cardinal Pole arrived in this realm in November 1554.

This is an evaluative phrase which links the contextual knowledge to the source.

This is also an evaluative phrase, used to link the next piece of contextual knowledge to the source.

Response A

The source argues that the restoration of Catholicism was popular in the north, with old services and practices restored. There is certainly some truth in this, as even further south an altar was rebuilt in Melton Mowbray in Leicestershire and masses were said, and moreover even in London where Protestantism was further entrenched parishes rushed to restore Catholicism, with one church putting up an altar as early as 23 August.

This is precise contextual knowledge used to support the point.

This is the next piece of contextual knowledge, following the linking phrase 'and moreover'.

Response B

The source argues that the restoration of Catholicism was popular in the north, with old services and practices restored. An altar was

> rebuilt in Melton Mowbray in Leicestershire and masses were said, and in London parishes rushed to restore Catholicism, with one church putting up an altar as early as 23 August. A requiem mass was heard in Bishopsgate, London, and churchwardens' accounts show that Latin service books were bought.

Although this response contains more contextual knowledge than Response A, this knowledge is not being used to evaluate the source. There are no evaluative words and the knowledge is not linked to the source to explain whether the view in the source is valid or not. Evaluation is only implied by what has been written, and without clear evidence of evaluation the response will not reach the top levels.

The answer might go on to explain how much was spent on restoring the fabric of churches so that they could perform the restored services, but again this needs to be directly linked to the source.

Before you start writing, it is important to ask yourself: 'What do I know that either challenges or supports the view in the source or interpretation?' In evaluating primary sources, it may be helpful to draw up a table to ensure that you cover both provenance and contextual knowledge and that you reach an overall judgement about the source. Table 4.2 gives an example of how you might do this.

Table 4.2 Evaluating primary sources

Source	Provenance	Knowledge that supports the view	Knowledge that challenges the view	Judgement
A				
B				

In the final column you should aim to reach a judgement about the source, based on the provenance and its impact on the reliability of the source and on your contextual knowledge. In light of those considerations, do you trust the view the source is offering?

A similar approach is required when you are dealing with secondary sources or interpretations, but in this case you will not be required to comment on the provenance of the interpretation as only AO3 is being assessed. You are assessing the view in the passage, not its provenance. It is also quite likely that you will not have heard of the author and would not be able to say anything useful about them. It is worth remembering, therefore, that you should not comment on who wrote the book or interpretation.

This means that really the only way you can test the view of a historian about an event is by applying your knowledge to the view. This is probably less daunting if you have contextual knowledge that supports the view being offered. It might seem more daunting as an

! Common pitfall

Ensure that when you analyse and evaluate primary sources, you both consider their provenance and apply contextual knowledge. Many responses do just one of these, which limits the level they can reach.

A-level student to challenge the views of famous historians. However, you should remember that historians are selective when they write. They may choose evidence to support their point of view, and ignore or downplay material that does not fit their line of argument.

Annotated example: analysing an extract

You are given the extract below about the decision to annihilate the Jews, taken from a secondary source. You are asked to consider how far this (and another interpretation you have been given) support the view that the Holocaust was mainly the result of a long-term plan by Hitler to eliminate the Jews.

The first thing you should do is work out what view is expressed by the interpretation about whether the Holocaust was the result of a long-term plan. The annotations show how you could do this.

Extract 2

If the language of the rabid anti-Semites was to be taken literally, then by 1939 the Jews had good reason to fear for their property, or their citizens' rights but also for their lives. This is not to imply that the inventors of the Final Solution had a clear idea before 1939 of how to solve the 'Jewish Question'. The only organisation to take a systematic approach was the SS and it came up with an emigration programme. A revised version of the programme re-emerged in 1940/1 in the plan to ship all Jews to Madagascar for resettlement. Heydrich called this idea the 'territorial final solution'. However, the outbreak of war and its subsequent escalation into total war seriously weakened the Jews' chances of survival. The military victories in the east and west suddenly added several millions of Jews to the number who had been unable to leave the Reich before September 1939. Any 'resettlement' plans had now become a major logistical and bureaucratic operation, the size of which helped to tip the scales in favour of physical annihilation. However, before this possibility could be seriously contemplated, there were also the psychological barriers to be removed. Resettlement plans were still being discussed as late as the spring of 1941.

Taken from V. R. Berghahn, *Modern Germany*, Cambridge University Press, 1982)

This suggests that there were no long-term plans for annihilation.

This suggests that the Holocaust was a response to the war and its escalation.

This reinforces the idea that it was the war that led to the Holocaust.

By analysing the extract as shown above, you would be able to explain the view of the interpretation about the issue in the question. However, to reach the highest levels you would still need to evaluate it by applying contextual knowledge. The annotations below show how you could do this.

Extract 2 (repeated)

Although this was given serious consideration, it should be remembered that such a policy would probably have led to their annihilation given the conditions they would have found there. This suggests that the Nazis were looking at ways to eradicate the Jews, and were not really concerned about resettlement, as is also suggested by the conditions within ghettoes.

If the language of the rabid anti-Semites was to be taken literally, then by 1939 the Jews had good reason to fear for their property, or their citizens' rights but also for their lives. This is not to imply that the inventors of the Final Solution had a clear idea before 1939 of how to solve the 'Jewish Question'. The only organisation to take a systematic approach was the SS and it came up with an emigration programme. A revised version of the programme re-emerged in 1940/1 in the plan to ship all Jews to Madagascar for resettlement. Heydrich called this idea the 'territorial final solution'. However, the outbreak of war and its subsequent escalation into total war seriously weakened the Jews' chances of survival. The military victories in the east and west suddenly added several millions of Jews to the number who had been unable to leave the Reich before September 1939. Any 'resettlement' plans had now become a major logistical and bureaucratic operation, the size of which helped to tip the scales in favour of physical annihilation. However, before this possibility could be seriously contemplated, there were also the psychological barriers to be removed. Resettlement plans were still being discussed as late as the spring of 1941.

This appears to be valid as pressure on the Jews had been increased with events such as Kristallnacht, the Nuremberg Laws and Hitler's speech to the Reichstag in January 1939.

This is certainly true as the invasion of Poland and then in 1941 of Russia brought millions of Jews under Nazi control. Such numbers would have been very difficult to resettle and an attempt to do so would have seriously disrupted the war effort.

This was certainly true as Britain, with its navy, would not allow the transportation of Jews to Madagascar.

There are obviously other points made in the interpretation that a response could pick up on and apply contextual knowledge to, but the crucial point is that the historical knowledge is linked directly to the interpretation through a series of evaluative words and phrases.

The same approach applies at both AS and A-level. If you are doing the OCR AS Unit 2 paper where you are given a short quote from a historian, it is important to adopt exactly the same approach. You must link the contextual knowledge to part of the interpretation; otherwise any link will just be implied and your answer will not score highly.

There are a few words of caution to remember when evaluating secondary sources or interpretations:

→ The knowledge that you apply must be both accurate and relevant to the issue.

→ It must be linked to the secondary source or interpretation to show that it either supports or challenges the view.

→ Large amounts of knowledge should not simply be written down after a source with no comment suggesting whether that knowledge makes the view of the source more or less valid.

→ The link between the contextual knowledge and the secondary source or interpretation should be clearly expressed by using an evaluative word or phrase.

Developing an evaluative vocabulary

As we have seen in the previous section, evaluative words are crucial in linking your contextual knowledge to a secondary source or interpretation. It might therefore be helpful to build up a store of such words and phrases during your course so that you become accustomed to using them before the exam. Although this might appear rather mechanical, it can help you to demonstrate the skills that the higher levels of the mark schemes require. It will also be helpful if you have to evaluate either secondary sources or interpretations in your coursework (see p 58).

The words, phrases and structures in Table 4.3 may be helpful.

> **Exam tip**
>
> Do not write for long stretches when evaluating a secondary source without using evaluative words to link your contextual knowledge back to the source or interpretation.

Table 4.3 Evaluative vocabulary

Words and phrases	Sentence structures
However	This is supported by…
Conversely	This is challenged by…
Although	The view is valid because…
On the other hand	The view is questionable because…
opposes	This interpretation can be criticised because…
illustrates	This view is supported by the example of…
confirms	His/Her argument rests on the premise that…but…
endorses	Too much significance is given to…whereas…
refutes	The historian makes a generalisation that excludes…
conflicts with	There is sometimes no evidence to support a claim, for instance….

You should know

> **Read the source carefully to work out what it says about the specific issue in the question.**

> **Do not simply explain the view of the source or interpretation about the issue in the question as that will not get you into the higher levels of the mark scheme.**

> **Evaluate a primary source by considering its provenance and applying contextual knowledge to judge the validity of the view expressed.**

> **Avoid discussing the provenance of a secondary source or interpretation in your answer.**

> **Use evaluative words, such as 'valid' or 'challenges', to link your contextual knowledge directly to a source or interpretation.**

5 Coursework

Learning objectives

> To know the requirements for coursework and the assessment objectives associated with it
> To be able to choose a good question that is manageable and has sources available
> To know why it is important to start researching for your essay as soon as you can and to identify relevant sources
> To be able to deconstruct the question so that you can focus on particular elements for your research
> To be able to construct a plan so that you can write up your coursework
> To be able to carry out self-assessment of the work
> To know how to keep a log and understand its importance

Coursework forms an integral part of A-levels for all the examination boards and is worth 40 marks out of 200 or 20% of the final mark. However, each of the examination boards has slightly different requirements and you should ensure that you are aware of these before embarking on this element of the course (see the Exam board focus section for more information; further guidance is also provided in the History Coursework Workbooks published by Hodder Education).

The coursework will provide you with the opportunity to explore in greater depth an area of interest that you have or have developed during the course. There are some limitations as to what you can choose, which are explained in the last section, and you may need to have your title approved by the examination board. If your title does need to be approved it is a good idea to submit it as soon as you can so that you have the green light to start work — it would be frustrating to have spent time working on a title only for it to be rejected.

What sort of essay is required?

The word limit

All of the examination boards require the essay to be somewhere between 3,000 and 4,000 words in length. In terms of assessment objectives (AOs), they all test AO1 and AO3, but Edexcel does not test AO2. These are important issues to bear in mind when considering a title. For example, you might consider whether there are sufficient historical debates to enable you to access the high levels for AO3, or whether you can obtain enough primary sources to reach the high levels for AO2.

The word limit is for your benefit. If you wrote less than the amount stated in the guidance it is unlikely that you would deal with the topic in sufficient depth, but if you wrote substantially more then experience has shown that there would be a tendency for you to describe developments or events in greater depth rather than focusing on the key skills of analysis and judgement. The skills that you need to demonstrate can be shown effectively within the word limit.

The word limit will also have an impact on the topic and question you choose. Is there enough material to write 3,000–4,000 words which are well focused? Is there too much material? These are important considerations when choosing your topic and question.

Style of writing

You must remember that it is an essay and therefore requires continuous prose. There is no need for a pretentious style, but it will need to flow as a piece of writing. Unless they are required, avoid the use of bullet points and subheadings.

There are no specific marks available for the quality of English, but as you have the chance to use a spellchecker do take advantage of it, and as you have plenty of time, do check for typos and misspellings. You can also help the marker by producing your essay in a clear and readable font, such as Arial 12 — but check whether your examination board has a specific requirement.

This is an academic piece of work, something you might discuss at a university interview or in your university application, so the wording of the title and the style should be academic rather than journalistic. It might be helpful to think of a good, clear textbook as a model for your writing. Footnotes are usually expected when sources are referred to and there should also be a bibliography.

Essays can describe events or offer a series of explanations, but as we have seen in Chapter 3, the higher marks are reserved for sustained and supported judgements which do not simply explain what happened and why. In making these judgements you may need to use and evaluate a range of sources which may be primary, secondary or both.

✓ Exam tip

Take care in choosing your title and ensure that you will be able to write enough and that the question will allow you to demonstrate all the high-level skills needed for a high mark.

Planning and time

You will have a considerable amount of time to do the coursework and the temptation might be to leave it until the end. However, not only is the scope much greater than for class essays but, given the time that you have, the examination boards will expect you to have done a lot more research. Because you have time to check and redraft your work, they will also expect you to be consistently focused on the question and to show a greater depth of analysis and evaluation than in an examined unit.

Choosing a title

If you can choose your own title, think of something in which you are interested. This is particularly important because, as it is worth 40 marks or 20% of your A-level, you really need to spend between 2 and 3 hours per week on it. We have already suggested that it needs to deliver the requirements of the mark scheme and that it should be manageable within the word limit. It does not require such detailed research that it is more suitable for a PhD thesis and it is not expected that you have access to a university library or extremely specialised sources. It is better to choose a topic that you understand, as complex topics can simply make too many demands on your time.

Choosing your title is very important as your essay will be marked against the title, that is in terms of how well you have answered your question. Make sure therefore that it is a question that can actually be answered and will allow you to show the right skills. Spending time thinking about the title is time well spent. Even ensuring that you get the command word right is vital. It might be helpful to look at some of the command words and phrases used in your examination papers, such as 'Assess', 'To what extent', 'How far' or 'How important'.

Checking for sources and interpretations

At this stage it is also a good idea to make sure that there are sufficient accessible sources. Some questions appear to be fascinating, but there is just not the material available. It is better to discover that at the start than after a few months of work when you run out of material.

It is also a good idea to unpack the question at an early stage as again this will help to ensure that the question will work. Consider the following question:

How effective was opposition to Hitler?

Your initial reading and research will soon make clear that opposition from all sides was not very effective, even from the army at the end as he was not overthrown. This will suggest that there is unlikely to be much of a debate for you to access AO3. However, the reading might have identified reasons why the opposition was ineffective and this could become the focus of the essay. You could keep the topic in which you are interested, but slightly change the focus of the question. It is therefore important that in the early weeks you do some preliminary research to make sure the question will work.

An early search for sources and interpretations will also allow you to identify the issues and factors that you are going to discuss in your answer.

If you need to use primary sources then you will have to find primary evidence that supports the different explanations you have found. There are a range of places you can look:

→ your school or college history department
→ within secondary texts
→ published collections of sources
→ the internet, by searching for primary sources on your topic

Having done such a search you can be certain there is sufficient material available for your question (or change your question if not).

Your research will need to be focused as there is likely to be a great deal of material out there relevant to your topic. It is absolutely vital that when you read the material you are focusing on what it

> **! Common pitfall**
>
> If you chose the essay title 'Describe the main events of the Russian Revolution', it would not score highly as 'Describe' is not a good command word. Nor would the title 'What were the main events of the Russian Revolution?' as you could just list them.

> **✓ Exam tip**
>
> Spend time checking that you will be able to find sufficient primary and secondary sources for your topic and question before you begin.

> **✓ Exam tip**
>
> In the early weeks it is a good idea to compile a list of resources that you can use and check that they are available. In particular, ensure that there are a range of interpretations as this will be important in reaching the higher levels for AO3.

tells you about the issues in your question and how the evidence might be used. For example, if you were answering 'How successful were the Nazi aims for women?', it would be helpful to start by researching what those aims were before then finding evidence as to whether they achieved each of them. This kind of approach will help to make the research more manageable as you will not be trying to research the whole question from the very start.

✓ **Exam tip**

It will be much easier to tackle your research if you break your question down into a series of smaller questions which you then focus on.

Keeping a research log

Some examination boards require you to keep a research log and will provide guidance as to how it should be kept. Even if your board does not require this, it is worth doing. A research log can be useful in helping you to keep a record of your ideas and sources. Later on you will need to reference everything you have used and the log can help with that task. Similarly you might have a good idea but forget it because you did not jot it down, and the log can help you overcome this. It will also help your tutor or teacher see the progress you have made and can be used as evidence to show that the essay is your own work. An example of how you might set out a research log is shown in Table 5.1.

Table 5.1 Example of a research log format

Date	Work done Resources found	Key ideas from the work/resources	How does it help? What next?

Using primary and secondary sources

Depending on your examination board you may need to integrate primary and secondary sources into your essay and evaluate them, that is make judgements about their value in answering your question. You will already have become accustomed to doing this for primary sources as discussed in Chapter 4. That chapter also gives advice on evaluating interpretations, which appear in the units of all the examination boards, and again you will need to do the same thing for your coursework. The only difference is that you have to select the evidence, unlike in the examination, and integrate your critical treatment of the sources into the essay. But as with the examined units you will need to:

→ read sources (primary and secondary) and understand how they relate to the issue in your question

→ look at the provenance of primary sources and assess how it impacts on their validity as evidence about the issue in your question

→ use your own knowledge of the period to assess the validity of the view of the source, either primary or secondary

! **Common pitfall**

When you are dealing with secondary sources you should check what your examination board requires. You may just need to cover a range of issues. On the other hand, you may need to evaluate different schools of history, such as traditionalist or revisionist, or the views of named historians.

In handling secondary sources or interpretations there are three possible ways that you could use them:

→ Describe the interpretation.

→ Explain the interpretation.

→ Evaluate the interpretation.

A quick look at the mark scheme will show where the high-level marks are to be achieved and you should ensure that you focus on that.

You might find it helpful to construct a series of tables that allow you to evaluate primary and secondary sources so they are available when it comes to writing up your essay. They could take the format suggested in Table 5.2. This can also be adapted for assessing the provenance of primary sources.

> ### ✓ Exam tip
>
> When you come to use the interpretation in your essay, ensure you link your knowledge to the interpretation. This is best done through a range of evaluative words and phrases. This will show clearly that you have assessed the validity of the view. It is worth building up a list of evaluative words and phrases during the course (see Table 4.3 on p. 54 for suggestions) as this will also help you with the examined units where AO3 is tested.

Table 5.2 Evaluation of sources

Argument in the source	Knowledge I have that supports the argument	Knowledge I have that challenges the argument	Judgement

It should now be clear that coursework is just an extension of the skills that you have covered for your examined units, but on a bigger scale and with greater depth expected because of the time you have available.

Writing up the coursework

As discussed earlier, you do not need to learn any new skills for the coursework as they will have been developed in your examined units. However, the coursework involves a much longer essay and you will need to make sure that you answer the specific question you have asked. You will have had ample time to think about the issues and to find plenty of relevant material. No one book will provide you with a ready-made answer: there is no shortcut to this, so it is crucial to get started in good time. You will need to have completed the research so that you are in a position to start writing up the work.

Thinking about the issues

As with any essay, you will need to make sure that you have arguments both for and against your question and also evidence to support both sides of the argument. As you are doing this it is important to think about the issues. This is so that when you plan your essay you have really thought through your line of argument and know the direction the essay is going to take. This will also help to ensure that you write relevantly for the 3,000–4,000 words. You must make sure that everything you write is about the issues in your question and not just generally about the topic:

→ You will need to ensure that there are no parts of the essay where you lose focus on the actual question.

→ You will need to check that there are no descriptive parts.

→ You will need to ensure that you have covered different views and have not produced a one-way argument.

→ All of your arguments must be backed up by detailed and accurate knowledge.

→ Your conclusion must follow logically from the main body of the answer.

This should all look familiar as very similar points were made in relation to your examined long-essay units in Chapter 3.

Developing a plan

In planning your essay, it might be helpful to start with a spider diagram that identifies the issues you intend to discuss. This can then be developed by indicating the relative importance of the factors either by varying the lengths of the 'legs' or by numbering the legs. You should also draw links in between any of the factors where there are links. This should ensure that you have covered all the issues that are important in answering your question.

The next step is to outline:

→ the issues or factors you will cover

→ the arguments for and against each issue and the evidence you will use

Then it might be helpful to identify which primary and secondary sources will be added in and where.

A table structured like Table 5.3 might be helpful in doing this.

Table 5.3 Outline of issues, arguments and sources

Title:					
Issue	Evidence for	Evidence against	Primary sources	Secondary sources	Judgement about the issue

Higher-level responses will make judgements on each issue they discuss based on the evidence they have used and by evaluating either primary or secondary sources or both, so it is worth having those elements in your table. This table should give you the structure and outline you need to start writing and you can then refer to your notes to develop any of your ideas.

Writing the essay

The opening paragraph

As with your other essays, the opening paragraph should explain the question, but should also indicate why there might be different interpretations and briefly mention some of the evidence that might support these, before suggesting your own view about the question.

Avoiding narrative and description

As we saw with essay writing, narrative and descriptive writing do not score well so it is worth going back to Chapter 3 to check that you know what to avoid. There is an even greater tendency with 3,000–4,000 words to drift into description and this can soon take you out of the top level.

This is where paragraph-opening sentences that introduce an idea can play a crucial role and, along with the plan, help to keep you

 Exam tip

At this stage it might be helpful to go back to your question and check that you have covered all the implications. As with essay writing you should underline the key words and phrases in your title as this will help you to maintain focus.

Exam tip

Remember all the skills you learnt for writing essays, as the same apply for the coursework. Look back to Chapter 3 to refresh your memory.

focused. Unlike in the examination you have plenty of time to make sure that each of your opening sentences is introducing a relevant idea and not simply imparting information.

Discussion not explanation

You do need to answer the question you have set and therefore just explaining a list of reasons will not score high marks. You will need to weigh up the importance of the issues you discuss in relation to other explanations of an event. In developing your argument you will need to consider both sides of it and bring in primary and secondary sources to support or challenge them.

Checking

Do keep checking that you are focused on your question as otherwise you are likely to slip down the mark bands. Make sure that your writing is not becoming descriptive and that you are not starting to discuss the topic in a general way instead of focusing on the issues in the question. Ensure that you are answering the question you set and not a different one. Reread paragraphs and remove any material that is not relevant to the question.

Integrating sources

You will need to bring in source material, be it primary or secondary or both. You can use it to illustrate a point or support your argument, or you can evaluate it so that it supports or challenges your argument. It is the skill of evaluation that will score the highest marks. If you integrate sources into your answer they will not disrupt the flow of the essay and will add to the strength of your analysis.

Annotated example: integrating and evaluating sources

Below is an example of integrating primary and secondary sources into an answer and using contextual knowledge to evaluate them.

How far was the Pilgrimage of Grace a religious rising?

Dickens has dismissed the pilgrims' religious motive and accused them of being incapable of staging wars of religion. What seems to contradict this is that 9 out of 24 of the Pontefract Articles deal with religion. However, these Articles might have been used to disguise personal and political issues. They were produced not by the common people but by educated elites who had more than just religious grievances. Haigh has also argued that 'the economic concerns of the people and the legal and political concerns of the leaders could have been cloaked by the religious language of the Articles'. The economic stress of the north supports this view. The harvest of 1535 had been bad and the genuineness of the religious concerns of the Articles can be questioned since the banning of the sales of indulgences was not mentioned. However, the religious symbolism of the Pilgrimage, the obvious idealism of Aske shown when he was being questioned after his arrest and the appearance of religious concerns in the majority of the Pontefract Articles mean that it cannot be convincing to take such a strong line as Dickens does about the nature of the Pilgrimage.

Secondary sources	Primary sources	Own knowledge to evaluate

Judgement

It is helpful to make interim judgements as you write your essay and these should lead to an overall judgement based on the critical use you have made of the evidence. The question you have chosen should lead you to a judgement. Therefore a title like this one is not suitable:

Describe the Dissolution of the Monasteries.

Instead a title like the following is suitable:

'Financial motives were the most important reason for the Dissolution of the Monasteries.' How far do you agree?

To answer that question, you would need to make a clear judgement about the relative importance of financial motives. So in the course of the essay it will have been a good idea to make judgements about the importance of the other factors you have discussed. The conclusion will then allow you to bring together all the interim judgements to make an overall judgement about the question.

Footnotes and bibliography

Even if it is not part of the mark scheme you should include footnotes and a bibliography. It is good practice as you will be required to do this at university if you have to write dissertations and in any case you should acknowledge where you got your information from. It is wrong to claim for yourself ideas and knowledge that you have taken from other sources — that is called plagiarism.

All the works that appear in the footnotes should be in the bibliography. With a computer, footnotes are easy to do as the computer will ensure that they are in numerical order. However, be careful not to use footnotes to add extra information — if the information is important it should be in the essay.

Self-assessment

Although your teacher will be able to give you some guidance, they cannot mark drafts and return them to you for rewriting. This means that self-assessment becomes a vital tool in ensuring you have met the criteria of the mark scheme. It might be helpful to use the following checklist of questions as you check through your work.

> ✓ **Exam tip**
>
> Ensure your bibliography includes all the details for the items you have used:
> - For a book you will need the title and author; the page(s) you have used; and the place and date of publication.
> - For an article you should include the title and author of the article; and the title, volume and publication date of the journal.

> ✓ **Exam tip**
>
> It is a good idea to construct a bibliography as you go along because it is a record of all the works you have read or consulted in order to do the essay.

Checklist for coursework

- ☐ Have I related everything in my essay to the question?
- ☐ Have I assessed different explanations?
- ☐ Have I looked at both sides of the argument?
- ☐ Have I deleted passages that are only descriptive?
- ☐ Have I included interim judgements?
- ☐ Have I made an overall judgement in the conclusion?
- ☐ Have I used detailed knowledge to support my argument?
- ☐ Have I included primary sources?
- ☐ Have I used a range of primary sources?

☐ Have I explained the primary sources and used them to support an argument?

☐ Have I evaluated them?

☐ Have I referenced them in footnotes?

☐ Have I included named historians?

☐ Have I referenced the historians in the footnotes?

☐ Have I used a range of historians' views?

☐ Have I explained the views and used them to support the argument?

☐ Have I evaluated them?

It is worth using the highlight tool on the computer to identify analysis, judgement and evaluation both of issues and of sources. This will help you to see how consistently you are doing these important skills. You will then have the opportunity to go back and improve weaker elements.

You should know

- **Pick a topic that interests you and for which there is material available.**
- **Devise a question about which there is a debate.**
- **Plan your coursework and start early so that you have time to find your resources, read widely and plan carefully before you write it up.**
- **Identify relevant sources at the start of the process.**
- **Keep a research log as it will provide evidence that the essay is your own work, and will be a useful way to record references for your sources and a list of issues that you might want to consider in your answer.**
- **Plan your answer using a chart in the form of a table.**
- **Integrate primary and secondary sources into your writing.**
- **Make interim and overall judgements about the issues you discuss.**
- **Use self-assessment to check your work.**

6 Writing short and thematic essays for OCR

Learning objectives

> To understand the meaning of the command words and phrases that will be used
> To focus on the exact wording of the question
> To know how to structure a basic short-essay paragraph
> To know how to reach a supported judgement
> To develop your own writing style

The short essay

The majority of the essays that you write will be 'long answers' for which you will have about 40–45 minutes depending on whether you are doing the AS or A-level examination, which examination board you are with and which component or unit you are doing. However, for OCR A-level Unit 2, Papers Y201–224, you are required to answer a short-essay question on which you will spend about 15 minutes. One of the reasons why this type of question is set is to allow the examination paper to cover a wider range of the period you have studied so that you have not spent time learning a lot of material that is not examined. The question will come from a different part of the specification than the long essay.

Deconstructing the question

The short-answer questions have a common structure, illustrated in the annotated example below.

Annotated example: short-answer question

Which of the following was of greater importance in establishing the Nazi dictatorship?

(i) the Enabling Act

(ii) the Night of the Long Knives

Explain **your answer with reference to** both **(i) and (ii).**

Command words	Topic	Specific focus within the topic

Identifying the parts of the question before you start to write is very important. It will help you to remain focused on the question and ensure that everything you write is relevant and therefore gains you marks. By writing only what is relevant you are also more likely to keep to your timings and not write too much. In the example above, the question asks only about the Enabling Act and the Night of the Long Knives — although there were other events that helped establish the Nazi dictatorship you will not gain any marks by writing about them.

> ## ! Common pitfall
>
> Many candidates write all they know about the two issues in the question, in this example the Enabling Act and the Night of the Long Knives, but do not explain how they relate to the focus of the question, in this example how they helped in the establishment of the Nazi dictatorship.

Analysis vs description

It is important to understand the difference between analysing and explaining the importance of an issue and describing the issue.

The difference between...

Which of the following had the greater impact on the Russian economy during Stalin's rule?

(i) collectivisation

(ii) the first two Five Year Plans

Explain your answer with reference to both (i) and (ii).

Descriptive answer	Analytical answer
Collectivisation brought together a number of small farm units to form bigger farms. Collectivisation occurred in two phases: there was the so-called voluntary phase that lasted up to March 1930 and the forced phase that started at the beginning of 1931. Together the phases resulted in 98% of all peasant households in Russia working on collectives by 1941. In 1929 Russia produced nearly 67 million tonnes of grain and by 1939 this had reached 75 million tonnes. The number of tractors also rose during this period from 4,000 to 18,000...	Collectivisation had a significant impact on the Russian economy. If the figures for the rise in production before the Second World War are accurate it meant that more food was available to feed the growing urban workforce. The expansion in tractor production also suggests that industrial production was stimulated by the needs of the agricultural sector. However, it must also be remembered that collectivisation had some detrimental impacts on the economy. The persecution of the kulaks reduced the size of the labour force available to work the land...

Structuring short answers

You should aim to spend about 15 minutes on the short-answer question and aim to write three or four paragraphs. The first paragraph should briefly explain the two issues and their significance and offer your view as to which is the more important with a reason. The second and third paragraphs should be similar in that you discuss the significance or importance of the two issues, factors or people in the question, with a paragraph on each. The final paragraph should reach a supported judgement where you explain which of the two was the most significant or important.

Do not waste time with a long introduction where you describe the event. It adds little to the answer, wastes valuable time and will not score marks.

In each of your main paragraphs, try to make three or four separate points about the importance or otherwise of the event, issue or

> ## ✓ Exam tip
>
> You do not need to write a comparative answer where you compare the importance or significance of the issues point by point. This approach will score just as well, but is much harder to organise and takes longer. It is better to write separate paragraphs on each issue — you will still score just as well.

person you are discussing. This should ensure that you have sufficient time to explain the point, but also ensure that you give sufficient coverage to the issue. Through practice you should know roughly how many words you can write in the time allowed so that you can work out how many words or lines you can write for each paragraph. This should also ensure that you do not spend too much time on one issue and run out of time on the question or spend too long on this question leaving insufficient time for the long essay.

The annotated example below shows how you might structure a paragraph about one of the issues.

Annotated example: paragraph in a short essay

Which of the following was of greater importance in establishing the Nazi dictatorship?

(i) the Enabling Act

(ii) the Night of the Long Knives

Explain your answer with reference to both (i) and (ii).

The Enabling Act, passed in March 1933, was crucial in establishing the Nazi dictatorship, as it transferred full legislative powers to the chancellor, Hitler, and his government for four years, thus establishing a dictatorship. This Act therefore meant that Parliament and parliamentary legislation became an irrelevance, with the Reichstag voting away its own existence. However, in actually voting it away, rather than having this imposed by force, it gave the establishment of dictatorship the appearance of legality even though members of the Reichstag had been intimidated to ensure its passage. The Act also helped to strengthen Hitler's position within the cabinet, as the president's approval was no longer needed for passing legislation, further adding to Hitler's power. It also gave Hitler the power to revise the constitution and removed any doubts that the middle classes had about the legality of the Nazi takeover, as everything appeared to have been done legally.

The first point about the Act's importance is explained.

The point about its importance is developed.

A further point about its importance is suggested.

An additional point about its importance in establishing the dictatorship is outlined.

A further point is outlined.

The example above makes three or four points about the importance of the Enabling Act and how it helped in establishing the dictatorship. Some are explicitly explained, while others suggest that it was important in gaining support for the regime as it made the establishment appear legal and this appealed to the middle class. What is important is that the material is constantly linked back to the actual question of 'establishing the Nazi dictatorship'.

Analysis and judgement

A quick look at the examination board mark scheme for this kind of question will show you that descriptive answers and those without a judgement will score very few marks. Therefore these are not 'easy' questions — they require the same level or quality of analysis and judgement that would be expected in a long essay if you are to reach the higher levels. For each point you make, you should ensure that you show how or why it was important or significant.

If you are unsure how to analyse the point you have made, there are some useful questions that you can think about:

→ In what ways is the point important or significant?
→ In what ways is the point a limitation?
→ What is the impact of the point?
→ Why is the point important or significant?

The following sentence starters should help to ensure that you move beyond mere description. You will create your own as you become accustomed to these questions and your writing style develops.

→ X was important because...
→ X was more significant than Y because...
→ X should be considered of greater significance as it...
→ However, it should not be forgotten that there were limits to the importance of X as...
→ The impact of X was far greater than that of Y because...
→ Although X was important in the short term, Y was of greater significance in the long term because...
→ Both X and Y were important as...

Even if you have explained and analysed the two issues in the question, you will still attain only the lower levels unless you reach a supported judgement as to which is the more important or significant. However, simply stating that (i) is more important than (ii) is not a judgement, it is an assertion. You need to explain why it is more important:

→ Why do you think it is more important?

→ What is your evidence to support your claim?

In considering what makes a strong judgement, we will return to the question about the Enabling Act and the Night of the Long Knives and look at the final paragraph.

Annotated example: final paragraph in a short essay

Which of the following was of greater importance in establishing the Nazi dictatorship?

(i) the Enabling Act

(ii) the Night of the Long Knives

Explain your answer with reference to both (i) and (ii).

The opening sentence establishes a view as to which event is the more important.

The reason why the Enabling Act is more important is explained.

The argument is balanced and there is awareness of the importance of the Night of the Long Knives, but even this is qualified.

> Although both events were important in establishing the Nazi dictatorship, the Enabling Act was more significant as it enabled Hitler to embark on a policy of Gleichschaltung, and create the one-party state by early 1934. This allowed Hitler to remove potential opposition in nearly every walk of life, including trade unions and other political parties; thus it was more significant in removing a range of opposition than the Night of the Long Knives. The only exception to this was the army, and the Night of the Long Knives was the event that won Hitler their support, but this simply completed the task begun by the Enabling Act. It is also unlikely that Hitler would have been able to undertake the Night of the Long Knives without the power and confidence he had gained from the Enabling Act, which again suggests that it was the most important event as it was the basis of his dictatorship and helped to take Hitler from the position of chancellor to that of Führer.

The opening suggests that the focus in the question has been addressed.

The argument as to why the Enabling Act is more important is reinforced and developed.

The example given above reaches a judgement that one event was more important than the other. However, for this type of question you can also argue that (i) is more important in one particular respect while (ii) is more important in another respect. That will also score well provided you support your argument. Remember there is no right or wrong argument, provided you can support your claim.

The thematic or synoptic essay

The thematic essay is a particular feature of OCR A-level Unit 3 (see p. 90). These essays require you to cover the whole period you have studied which will be a minimum of 100 years long. Although all the skills that you have already learned still apply to this paper, there is one further skill that you will need to develop if you are to reach the higher levels, known as synthesis.

In just the same way as your other essays, the answers for this paper will need to be analytical, with a consistent focus on the question, and show a substantiated judgement. However, there are also some differences. The title of the unit, 'Thematic study', makes it clear that the essays should be approached thematically and not chronologically. This type of approach will make it much easier for you to demonstrate the key skill of synthesis.

What is synthesis?

Synthesis is the bringing together of material from across the 100 years you have been studying and, most importantly, making links and connections between different parts of the period. In other words, you will be comparing and explaining similarities and differences across your period of study. It will not be enough to simply list examples from across the period in each paragraph; you must make direct comparisons, with explanations, between the examples you use. This means that you need to consider these questions:

→ In what ways (how) are the events, issues or people similar or different?

→ Why are they similar or different?

You do not need to make comparisons across the whole period in every paragraph, but during the course of the essay that should be covered.

The difference between...

Compare the two essay paragraphs below. They show a similar level of knowledge used and analysis, but only the one on the right shows synthesis. The question is as follows:

How far did ineffective leadership explain the failure of Tudor rebellions?

No synthesis	Synthesis
One of the reasons for the failure of the rising of the northern earls was certainly weak leadership. The earls had to be pressed by their wives into undertaking the rising and were therefore reluctant leaders, which would not have given potential supporters much confidence to join the rising and may explain the small numbers the rebellion attracted. The earls had been driven into rebellion out of despair and financial hardship and they had not developed a coherent plan for the rising, which was another reason for its failure. The leadership of Thomas Wyatt was a factor in the failure of the 1554 rising. He failed to advance rapidly on London, instead seizing Cooling	Leading a rebellion was a great responsibility, particularly when the numbers involved were large or the longer a revolt lasted. Ineffective leadership was a factor in the failure of a number of rebellions. There is little doubt that age was a factor in the qualities of a leader: while Simnel was too young, Northumberland and Westmorland were too old and this would have done little to inspire loyalty or provide the charisma needed to lead a major rebellion. Leaders who were indecisive or lacked strategy were also less likely to be effective. Wyatt was indecisive and failed to advance quickly on London when he might have succeeded. Similarly, the northern earls had no clear plan

Castle, which allowed Mary to prepare and fortify London Bridge. Wyatt's delay also had an impact on his forces and lowered their morale, which may also have been a factor in their failure. The leadership of Simnel was also a factor in the failure of his rebellion. Although he claimed to be the Earl of Warwick, he was too young to lead a rebellion or inspire people to follow him and this may explain why the rebellion attracted limited support. He was not physically strong or intimidating and lacked the charisma needed to inspire others.

and not only failed to realise how long it would take to march to Tutbury to free Mary Queen of Scots, but were also unaware that she had been moved. Ineffective leaders were also more likely to fail as they could attract little support or the wrong type of support. The northern earls and Simnel were unable to attract support because of their poor organisation. While the northern earls lacked funds to pay supporters, with the result that 600 promptly deserted, Simnel failed to realise that the presence of Irish nobles and their 'wild tenants' would discourage many English from joining as his force made its way south from Lancashire.

Comments:

This response simply lists and explains three ineffectual leaders: the northern earls, Wyatt and Simnel. No link or comparison is made between them.

There is some argument here; knowledge is accurate and relevant; and there is some analysis of how the failings of each leader led to failure. However, there is no judgement about leadership or comparison with other issues.

Comments:

This response compares the leadership of the three rebellions and shows synthesis, explaining a range of similarities and linking them back to the actual question.

In this response the level of knowledge is sufficient to support the argument and it is used, not just 'dumped' in the answer.

The strongest answers would go on and compare 'ineffective leadership' with other factors in order to reach a judgement about the most important reason for the failure of Tudor rebellions.

You should know

> It is important to deconstruct any question before starting to write your answer.
> In a short-answer question, do not waste time writing a long introduction where you describe the event.
> Short-answer questions require a judgement as AO1 asks for 'substantiated judgements'.
> A judgement needs to be supported by evidence — otherwise it is just an assertion.
> It is important to relate your explanation back to the actual issue in the question.
> Merely describing the two events or issues in a short-answer question will score low marks.
> For Unit 3 essays, you need to show the skill of synthesis, making comparisons across the period you have studied.

7 Exam skills

Learning objectives

> To develop effective revision strategies and techniques
> To know how to plan and structure an essay in exam conditions
> To be able to choose the right question quickly
> To know how to manage your time in the exam room

Much of the advice in the earlier part of this book has been designed to help you write essays during your course. However, things are a little different under exam conditions where time is at a premium. Under such circumstances you cannot spend a long time planning and drafting those vital opening sentences.

However, you should not leave the development of exam skills until you start your final revision. These skills can be developed during your course and you should be practising them on a regular basis so that they become second nature. You will probably have been doing essays under timed conditions for some time and that certainly provides the opportunity to develop the planning, timing and writing skills you will need in the exam room.

The same is true for revision: you should be revising the topics as you go through the course rather than just filing a completed topic and forgetting about it. Revisiting it during the course will certainly put you in a stronger position when you start your more intensive revision programme nearer the exam.

Before the exam

When you finish being taught a topic, do not simply put away your notes and work from that topic in your files and forget about them until you start revising. First, make sure they are organised as that will save you a considerable amount of time when you start revising and you will also have a better idea of the order they should be in when the topic is still fresh in your mind.

Second, go back over topics you have finished on a regular basis. Few students do this but it can make a big difference. If you do not revisit a topic you will forget most of what you have learnt and then when you start the final revision process you will be starting from a much lower base. Try and go back over topics every month, even if all you do is reread your notes, so that when you start your final revision you have a much better base from which to start.

It is also important to plan a revision programme. Again, do not leave this until the last minute. Examination board websites provide

 Exam tip

Make a list of the topics you have to revise for the exam and keep a record of each time you revisit them and the date. This will help ensure that you give equal time to all topics and encourage you to keep going back to topics.

the dates and times of exams well in advance, so go to them and make a note of the details. Knowing when your exam is will help to focus your mind and it does not make the time pass any more quickly.

You should know the structure of your exam, how many papers there are, how long each paper is, how many questions you will have to answer, the nature of those questions and the choices you will have. Further guidance on this is provided in the Exam board focus section.

Ensure that your notes are organised, and do this as you go along. You do not want to begin revising and discover that your notes are not in order or, even worse, that you cannot find some of them. Make sure you will be ready to start your revision programme without wasting valuable time sorting and organising your notes.

Revision techniques

Your revision will be much more productive if you take an active approach rather than trying to learn by heart large amounts of factual material. Simply looking at your notes and trying to learn them or reading them through time and time again will not be very productive. After no more than 10 minutes of that you are likely to find that you cannot remain focused and that you are staring at a page of words that have very little meaning — you just will not be taking in very much.

Active revision will require you to invest in a few things:
→ A3, A4 and A5 paper
→ coloured pencils, pens and a set of highlighters
→ index cards

A number of active methods for revision are described below.

Summaries

One of the best starting points for each topic you have to revise is to summarise it on a sheet of A3 paper. There are a number of ways to do this. Here are some suggestions:

→ Read your notes carefully and extract the really important points. You can do this in a spider diagram.
→ Write down on the spider diagram what you can remember, then go to your notes and check that you have included all the important points.
→ Once you are certain you have all the important points, you can do it again without notes to test yourself, or even do it on A4 or A5 paper so you really do have to summarise the information concisely.

This kind of approach will help you to identify gaps in your knowledge. Then you can focus on plugging those gaps rather than going back over what you already know.

Exam tip

Draw up a timetable for revision before the start of your revision programme. Ensure you allocate equal time to each subject and to topics within each subject. Do not spend more than about 45 minutes on a topic in one session.

! Common pitfall

There is a tendency for candidates to focus on issues and topics with which they feel confident, leaving out those areas they find harder, but in the exam there may not be choice. Ensure that you cover everything and put in extra time on those areas where you are less confident.

Activity

Take one of your topics you are less confident about and read your notes through. Try to remember the really important points and create a spider diagram. Ensure you have no more than eight key points. Check these against your notes and repeat the exercise.

Essay plans

Once you are confident that you have enough knowledge about a topic, essay plans are a useful revision tool. You can use questions from the exam board website, from past papers or from key questions within the specification, or you can devise your own. If there are key questions within the specification, do plan answers to those as it will ensure that you have sufficient material available when you reach the exam room and that you have thought about the kinds of issues around which exam questions are likely to be set.

When planning answers, remember to think about the following:

→ What is your overall view about the question?
→ What issues do you need to cover?
→ What would be the opening sentence for each paragraph?
→ What evidence would you use to support or challenge the idea you have raised in each opening sentence?

You can also go to essays you have written in the past and draw up a plan from what you wrote or devise a new plan. Think about the following:

→ What view did you put forward then?
→ Do you still agree with it?
→ Does it consider both sides of the argument?
→ Is the judgement developed?
→ How would you improve the essay?

As with summarising your notes, you can check your plan against your notes to ensure that you have not left anything crucial out. If you have, then you probably need to do some more work on the topic.

Activity

Before you start your revision programme, collect together all the possible essay questions for each topic. Thinking of new ones yourself is also a good way of revising.

Activity

When you have revised a topic, take two or three different questions that look at the topic from different angles. Produce essay plans for them, then check the plan against your notes and add in anything crucial that is missing.

At this stage it might be worthwhile doing full essay plans as outlined in Chapter 3 as this will help to ensure that you have enough material for the exam. However, it is also worth turning these into less detailed plans of the kind you can do under exam conditions. In exam conditions you should allow yourself about 5 minutes to plan each of the essays you are going to write and therefore cannot hope to produce anything as detailed as the ones you will have done in class.

It might helpful to think along the following lines:

→ What is going to be my line of argument?

→ What issues am I going to consider and in what order?

→ What is my argument going to be for each issue?

→ What knowledge do I have to support and challenge the argument?

→ What is my overall judgement?

Consider the following plan done under exam conditions, and compare it with the more detailed plan on page 31 in Chapter 3.

Annotated example: quick essay plan

How important was the Depression in bringing Hitler to power in January 1933?

View: unemployment gave Hitler popular support but it was backstairs intrigue that led ultimately to his appointment.

Point 1:

→ Unemployment led to support

→ Weimar's failure to deal with unemployment

→ Nazi performance at elections before and after Depression

→ Decline in support Nov. 1932

Point 2:

→ Weakness of Weimar

→ Cuts to benefit

→ Unable to deal with crisis

→ People look for alternatives

Point 3:

→ Hitler offers solution

→ Communists

Point 4:

→ Appeal of Hitler

→ Message

→ Propaganda

Point 5:
→ Backstairs intrigue
→ Role of Papen and control
→ Support on decline

On this plan you could draw arrows to link points and also alter the order in which you might tackle issues so that the essay flows. However, this type of plan might tend to just give you a list and no evaluation of the issue in the question. See the suggested alternative format below.

A better alternative would be to draw up this plan in two columns, one in which you argue for the point under discussion and another where you argue against it. It might look like Table 7.1.

Table 7.1 Quick essay plan with arguments for and against

Point	Arguments in favour of the point	Arguments against the point
1	• Weimar's failure to deal with unemployment • Nazi performance at elections before and after Depression	• Decline in support Nov. 1932
2	• Cuts to benefit • Unable to deal with crisis	• People look for alternatives, could be communists
3	• Hitler offers solution	• Communists
4	• Appeal of Hitler • Message • Propaganda	• Appeal of Hitler not evident pre-1929
5	• Backstairs intrigue • Role of Papen and control • Support on decline	• Without popular support Hitler would not have been considered

This type of approach ensures the pros and cons of each point are discussed and interim judgements are made, instead of just giving you a list with no evaluation of the issue in the question.

Obviously with practice you will become quicker at doing these plans. Remember that in the exam you can cross off points as you make them so you know what you have covered. They are your plans, so use them to help you.

Practice essays or parts of essays

It is likely that in the period leading up to revision and during the revision period you will have been doing revision essays. There is nothing to stop you doing extra ones or parts of ones and giving them to your teacher to mark. However, do them one at a time so that you get feedback before you do the next one. In that way you can avoid making the same mistake time and time again.

→ Redo essays to check that you have taken on board the comments made in the feedback. If you have done, your mark should have improved.

→ Practise some of the hard essays that have been set or essays on topics that you found more challenging. Not only will it be satisfying to do well, but it will also mean that in the exam you will not be put off by any of the questions.

→ Write parts of answers. You might want to write just the vital opening paragraph or a conclusion, or a single paragraph to ensure that you are considering both sides of an argument and reaching an interim judgement.

Activity

Using the essay questions that you have collected, practise writing opening paragraphs or conclusions for a range of questions as you revise each topic.

Revision or flash cards

You can create your own revision or flash cards to test yourself. On one side of the card you can put a question or a view or interpretation, and on the other side you can put the answer, for example:

Causes of the Dissolution of the Monasteries	Financial gain Allegiance to Rome Behaviour and corruption within monasteries Power Importance of Thomas Cromwell Protestant ideas

This flashcard lists a number of points that could be given as reasons for the Dissolution of the Monasteries. A flashcard need not contain every argument, just the ones that you think are important. You could also add examples to it if you wanted.

Asking someone to test you

A great way of checking your progress once you think you know the material is to get someone to test you. You can do this in two main ways:

→ If the person knows something about the topic, they can test you based on their knowledge. They might ask you to explain the causes of an event, explain an interpretation or work through the arguments for and against something.

→ If the person does not know your course then you can explain something to them, or you can give them your revision notes or essay plans and ask them to devise questions from those.

If you are unable to answer the questions or unable to explain something then you need to go back to the topic and revise it again.

Activity

Create your own podcasts or revision tutorials where you record six key points about an issue.

Remember there are also a range of professional podcasts available, such as Audiopi, which you can purchase and use.

Revising for source or interpretation questions

You might think that you do not need to do as much revision for source or interpretation questions as for the essay questions, as some of the material you will need will be in the sources or the interpretations. This is simply not true. You will need both to practise the required skills and to revise the content for those topics.

Once again it is important to keep your revision active. Obviously you can practise answering past or sample questions, but you can also fine-tune your skills. Here are some suggestions:

→ One of the key skills is to be able to identify the view in the source or interpretation, so it is a good idea to read sources or interpretations and practise doing this.
→ You should also look for evidence in the source or interpretation that supports the view it expresses.
→ Ask yourself what evidence you know of that supports or contradicts the view expressed in the source or interpretation.
→ In light of your evidence, write a judgement about the source or interpretation.

With source questions you are also likely to be required to comment on the provenance of the source. Here you need to think about how the provenance affects the view expressed. Try to avoid thinking in generic terms (e.g. 'it is from a diary and therefore will tell the truth'); instead, think about the specific source and try to write two or three sentences that comment on the provenance and how it impacts on the validity of the view expressed in the source.

! Common pitfall

When evaluating a primary source in the exam, many candidates comment either about the content or about the provenance, but not both — you need to think about both.

Activity

Using sources from past papers, identify what each source is saying about the issue in the question. Then find a brief quotation from the source to support your identification of the view expressed (i.e. to show you have identified it correctly).

Remember that many of the other revision methods suggested above also apply to source and interpretation questions, as you will need contextual knowledge to be able to evaluate sources and interpretations.

Revising for essay questions

In revising your material you should also focus on the skills you will need for the particular paper you are revising for. If you are revising for an essay paper then these are:

→ focusing on the issue in the question
→ analysing the issues
→ evaluating the relative importance of the issues and factors
→ reaching supported judgements

You will have studied all of the topics that make up the paper and so will be able to see the whole period in its broader context, rather than seeing topics in isolation. You will also have available all your earlier essays that you wrote during the course and these can be a valuable aid. A good activity can be to review some of the judgements you made previously about issues and questions, and consider whether, in light of further work that you have done, you would change your opinion.

Revision books

Hodder Education have produced a number of revision guides called *My Revision Notes* for many of the popular topics. These also contain activities to help you revise as well as checklists of topics so that you can ensure you have covered everything.

In the exam

There is plenty of generic advice available about preparing for exams and developing good revision habits: breaking up the day, the length of revision sessions, good sleeping and eating habits, exercise and so on. However, it is also worthwhile making sure that you have everything ready for the exam so that there are no last-minute panics. One obvious point is to make sure you know where the exam is and when it will take place — it is worth checking.

You will need to have a clear pencil case containing:

→ pens (make sure you are accustomed to using the pen you will use in the exam and that you have spares)

→ highlighters

→ pencils

Pencils and highlighters will allow you to identify clearly any parts of sources, key words in a question and so on.

Timing

We have talked about timing throughout the book, but do make sure you know how long you have got for each question. It is a good idea to note the timings on your question paper or on the front of the answer booklet and then (the hardest thing) stick to them. Remember you are likely to score more marks by ensuring you do all the questions you are supposed to, even if they are not quite finished, than if you spend an extra 5 minutes on one question at the expense of another.

You should be so accustomed to writing essays under timed conditions that you can judge the time well.

Picking the right question

On many parts of the examination papers you will have a choice of questions. You will need to allow yourself some time to read through the sections where there are optional questions and work out which question or questions you are going to do. Where there are parts to a question do ensure you can do the part that carries the most marks well.

Take care to choose a question that you can answer well and not one which is on a topic you like but which has a particular slant that

 Exam tip

Make sure you get plenty of practice writing answers, especially to essay questions, under timed conditions. This will give you a clear idea of how much you can expect to write.

will make it difficult for you to answer successfully. The key is to ensure that you can answer the specific question set and not simply write about the topic. Remember, the examiner wants to know your view about the question, not just what you know about the topic.

Activity

It is worth looking at complete past papers to ensure that on each you would know which question or questions to choose. From the available past papers identify which questions you would choose and explain why you would choose them.

Planning and structuring an essay

We have already given advice above on how to plan an essay under examination conditions. However, even though you have been told to do this there are many students who, fearing they will not finish the paper, rush straight into writing. The result is likely to be an answer without direction or structure. There are a number of reasons why spending 5 minutes planning will benefit you:

→ It will be a useful check on whether you can actually answer the question you have chosen.

→ It will give you the chance to organise your material so that there is a structure and coherence to your answer.

→ It will help you select material that is relevant instead of trying to write everything you know.

→ It should help to keep you focused on the actual question.

However, examiners are not looking for plans and there are no marks for them, so remember their purpose — they are for you, not the examiner. If you spend the time planning, make sure you use the plan.

After the exam

There is nothing you can do after an exam to change your performance, so there is no point in dwelling on what you have or have not written. If there are lessons that can be learned for future exams, for instance about timing or planning, that is useful, but worrying about what you wrote will not help — you need to move on and prepare for the next examination. Inquests with friends and teachers do not really help and may cause unnecessary anxiety which can impact on other exams that you still have to do.

You should know

> **Use a range of revision techniques to ensure that your revision is both active and effective.**

> **Make sure you put together all the stationery you will need in the exam, including a pen you are accustomed to writing with and some spares.**

> **Being strict with yourself about timings in an exam will bring benefits.**

> **Practising timings is crucial.**

> **Picking questions carefully and planning your answers is vital.**

> **Answer the question set — do not simply write everything you know about the topic.**

> **Once you have finished the exam, move on to preparing for the next one.**

Exam board focus

Learning objectives

> To become familiar with the structure of your exam(s)
> To know the length of your exam(s) and the number and type of questions you have to answer
> To understand how the marks are allocated
> To know where to find more information on your examination board

Each examination board has a different exam structure: the length and number of papers varies, as do the assessment weightings. This chapter will give you some information on how the AS and A-level history examinations are structured for your board. The information is relevant for the history courses taught from September 2017 onwards.

AQA
AS

All the information about this qualification can be found here: www.aqa.org.uk/subjects/history/as-and-a-level/ history-7041-7042

The features of the examination

AQA AS History consists of two papers, one a **breadth study** and one a **depth study**. Each paper is 1½ hours long. There are 50 marks available for each paper, giving a total of 100 marks.

Each paper covers a different type of study, with Component 1 focused on breadth and Component 2 focused on depth.

The structure of the examination

Although each of the examination papers consists of two sections, A and B, the nature of the questions and choice is different.

In **Component 1**, Section A has a compulsory question which tests your ability to analyse and evaluate the views of historians. Two contrasting interpretations linked to an issue are provided and you will have to assess them and reach a judgement as to which is the more convincing. This is worth 25 marks.

Section B of Component 1 has two questions and you are required to answer one. This is the essay section and you are required to analyse and evaluate the judgement in the question. This is worth 25 marks.

In **Component 2**, Section A has a compulsory question which tests your ability to analyse and evaluate primary sources. The question will require you to analyse the value of the sources and is worth 25 marks.

In Section B of Component 2, two questions are set and you have to answer one. This is the in-depth essay question and will take the form of a judgement which you will have to analyse and evaluate. It is worth 25 marks.

Marks and time

Tables 8.1 and 8.2 show the mark allocations for the questions in the two components, along with the approximate time you should allow per question. The kinds of wording typically used in the questions are also shown.

Table 8.1 Component 1 of AQA AS History

Question	Marks	Marks per AO	Approximate time per question	Typical question wording
1	25	AO3: 25	45 minutes	Which of these two extracts provides the more convincing interpretation?
2 OR 3	25	AO1: 25	45 minutes	To what extent do you agree/disagree… Explain why you agree/disagree with this view.

Table 8.2 Component 2 of AQA AS History

Question	Marks	Marks per AO	Approximate time per question	Typical question wording
1	25	AO2: 25	45 minutes	Which of these two sources is more valuable in explaining…
2 OR 3	25	AO1: 25	45 minutes	To what extent… How far… Explain whether you agree or disagree with this view.

A-level

All the information about this qualification can be found here: www.aqa.org.uk/subjects/history/as-and-a-level/history-7041-7042

The features of the examination

AQA A-level History consists of two examined components and a non-examined historical investigation. Components 1 and 2 each have an examination paper which is 2½ hours in length and consists of two sections. Components 1 and 2 each carry 80 marks while the historical investigation is worth 40 marks, giving a total of 200 marks.

You will study a British option for one of the two components and a non-British component for the other paper. There are two prohibited combinations because of overlap; these are listed in the specification.

As with AS each component focuses on a different element:

→ Component 1 assesses your **understanding of breadth and historical interpretations.** You will study one topic that covers at least 100 years from a choice of 11.

→ Component 2 assesses your **understanding of depth and the value of primary sources.** You will study one topic that covers approximately 50 years from a choice of 19.

The **historical investigation** is an extended piece of writing of between 3,000 and 3,500 words. The question, which AQA will need to approve, should be in the context of approximately 100 years and must not duplicate the content of Components 1 or 2. It should draw upon your investigation of both primary and secondary sources.

The structure of the examination

In **Component 1** there are two sections. Section A has a compulsory question which tests your ability to evaluate the views of historians. Three extracts are provided and you will have to identify the arguments and evaluate them using relevant knowledge and historical context. This question is worth 30 marks.

In Section B of Component 1, there are three essay questions and you will be required to answer two. Each essay will test your understanding over a period of approximately 20 years. However, to ensure that you show a breadth of understanding across the period the balance of the questions set will be as follows:

→ If Question 1 (the compulsory question in Section A) is set on Part 1 of the content, Section B will carry only one essay on Part 1 of the content or one that overlaps Parts 1 and 2, while two essays will be set on Part 2 of the content.

→ If Question 1 is set on Part 2 of the content, Section B will carry only one essay on Part 2 of the content or one that overlaps Parts 1 and 2, while two essays will be set on Part 1 of the content.

→ If Question 1 overlaps Parts 1 and 2 of the content, Section B will carry one essay from Part 1, one essay from Part 2 and a further essay from either part.

Each essay is worth 25 marks.

In **Component 2** there are two sections. Section A has a compulsory question which tests your ability to analyse and evaluate the value of primary sources. Three sources will be set and you will be required to consider their provenance and use your knowledge and understanding of the context to assess them. This question is worth 30 marks.

Section B of Component 2 consists of three essay questions and you will have to answer two. Each essay is designed to test your understanding in depth. Each question is worth 25 marks.

Component 3 is the historical investigation. You are required to produce an independently researched extended piece of writing of between 3,000 and 3,500 words which covers a period of approximately 100 years. It must not duplicate the content of the other components and will ensure that in your course of study you have covered a period of at least 200 years. The investigation is worth 40 marks.

Marks and time

Tables 8.3 and 8.4 show the mark allocations for the questions in the two components, along with the approximate time you should allow per question. The kinds of wording typically used in the questions are also shown.

Table 8.3 Component 1 of AQA A-level History

Question	Marks	Marks per AO	Approximate time per question	Typical question wording
1	30	AO3: 30	60 minutes including reading and planning time	Using your understanding of the historical context, assess how convincing the arguments in each of these three extracts are in relation to…
2, 3, 4 (choose TWO)	25 each	AO1: 25 each	45 minutes for each, including planning time	To what extent… How far… Assess the validity of this view.

Table 8.4 Component 2 of AQA A-level History

Question	Marks	Marks per AO	Approximate time per question	Typical question wording
1	30	AO2: 30	60 minutes including reading and planning time	Assess the value of these sources to the historian studying…
2, 3, 4 (choose TWO)	25 each	AO1: 25 each	45 minutes for each, including planning time	To what extent… How far… Assess the validity of this view.

Component 3

The historical investigation essay assesses all the assessment objectives and is weighted as follows:

→ AO1: 20 marks
→ AO2: 10 marks
→ AO3: 10 marks

Edexcel

AS

All the information about this qualification can be found here:
http://qualifications.pearson.com/en/qualifications/edexcel-a-levels/history-2015.html

The features of the examination

Edexcel AS History consists of two papers. Paper 1 is 2 hours
15 minutes long and is marked out of 60. Paper 2 is 1 hour
30 minutes long and is marked out of 40, giving a total of
100 marks.

Each paper covers a different type of study, with one focused on
breadth and the other on **depth**.

The structure of the examination

Paper 1 has three sections, A, B and C:

→ Section A comprises a choice of two essay questions and you
  must answer one. The questions will usually cover a period of at
  least 10 years and test cause or consequence.

→ Section B also comprises a choice of two essay questions where
  you must answer one. The questions will usually cover at least
  one third of the timespan of your option and will test any of the
  AO1 concepts.

→ Section C comprises one compulsory question where you will be
  required to analyse and evaluate two interpretations.

Paper 2 has two sections, A and B. Section A has a two-part
question which will require you to analyse and evaluate sources that
are primary or contemporary to the period you are studying. There
will be two sources and the two questions will be set on different
sources. In Section B there will be three essay questions and you
must answer one. They will test any of the AO1 objectives.

Marks and time

Tables 8.5 and 8.6 show the mark allocations for the questions in
the two papers, along with the approximate time you should allow
per question. The kinds of wording typically used in the questions
are also shown.

Table 8.5 Paper 1 of Edexcel AS History

Question	Marks	Marks per AO	Approximate time per question	Typical question wording
1 OR 2	20	AO1: 20	45 minutes to plan and write	Were... Explain your answer. To what extent…
3 OR 4	20	AO1: 20	45 minutes to plan and write	How significant… How far…
5	20	AO3: 20	45 minutes to read, plan and write	How convincing do you find the view…

Table 8.6 Paper 2 of Edexcel AS History

Question	Marks	Marks per AO	Approximate time per question	Typical question wording
1a, 1b	20	AO2: 20	45 minutes to read and write	Why is the source valuable to the historian for an enquiry about… How much weight do you give the evidence of Source X for an enquiry into…
2 OR 3 OR 4	20	AO1: 20	45 minutes to plan and write	How far… To what extent…

A-level

All the information about this qualification can be found here: http://qualifications.pearson.com/en/qualifications/edexcel-a-levels/history-2015.html

The features of the examination

Edexcel A-level History consists of three examined papers and a non-examined piece of coursework. Two of the examined papers are 2 hours 15 minutes in length and both of these carry 60 marks, while the other paper is 1 hour 30 minutes long and carries 40 marks. The coursework also carries 40 marks, which gives an overall total of 200 marks.

Each of the papers tests a different type of history. You should be aware that Papers 1 and 2 are grouped into eight 'routes' and the options are linked by themes. Each of these 'routes' comprises a mandatory Paper 1 and a choice of two options for Paper 2, of which you will study one. However, for Paper 3 there are a variety of options and the specification indicates permitted combinations to ensure that there is no content overlap, that you study at least 20% British history and that you cover a chronological range of at least 200 years.

The papers can be described as follows:

→ Paper 1 is focused on a **breadth study** with interpretations. There are eight options and you will study one.

→ Paper 2 is focused on a **depth study**. There are 16 options and you will study one.

→ Paper 3 is focused on **themes in breadth with aspects in depth**. There are 16 options and you will study one.

The **coursework** is an independently researched enquiry in which different interpretations are evaluated. The question is set by your centre and is based on an issue that has generated disagreement among historians.

The structure of the examination

The structure of each of the examination papers is different. Papers 1 and 3 consist of three sections, Sections A, B and C, while Paper 2 has two sections, Section A and B. Papers 1 and 3 are both 2 hours 15 minutes long, whereas Paper 2 is 1 hour 30 minutes long. The nature of the questions and the choice also differ among the papers.

Paper 1 requires you to answer three questions. You will choose one essay question from a choice of two for both Sections A and B and this will test your understanding of the period in breadth. For Section C you will answer one compulsory question which tests your ability to analyse and evaluate interpretations.

Paper 2 requires you to answer two questions, one from Section A and one from Section B. In Section A there is one compulsory question based on two sources that are either primary or contemporary to the period. You will be required to analyse and evaluate these. In Section B you will be required to answer one essay from a choice of two and this will test your understanding of the period in depth.

Paper 3 requires you to answer three questions, one from each of the sections, A, B and C. Section A consists of one compulsory question which requires you to analyse and evaluate a source that is primary or contemporary to the period you are studying. Section B consists of a choice of two essay questions that test your understanding of the period in depth. Section C consists of a choice of two essay questions that test your understanding of the period in breadth.

The **coursework** should be between 3,000 and 4,000 words in length. The coursework tests assessment objectives 1 and 3, weighted as follows:

→ AO1: 10 marks

→ AO3: 30 marks

Marks and time

Tables 8.7, 8.8 and 8.9 show the mark allocations for the questions in the three papers, along with the approximate time you should allow per question. The kinds of wording typically used in the questions are also shown.

Table 8.7 Paper 1 of Edexcel A-level History

Question	Marks	Marks per AO	Approximate time per question	Typical question wording
1 OR 2	20	AO1: 20	45 minutes to plan and write	How far… How successful…
3 OR 4	20	AO1: 20	45 minutes to plan and write	How significant… How accurate is it to say… To what extent…
5	20	AO3: 20	45 minutes to read, plan and write	How convincing do you find the view…

Table 8.8 Paper 2 of Edexcel A-level History

Question	Marks	Marks per AO	Approximate time per question	Typical question wording
1	20	AO2: 20	45 minutes to read and write	How far could the historian make use of Sources 1 and 2 to investigate…
2 OR 3	20	AO1: 20	45 minutes to plan and write	How far… To what extent…

Table 8.9 Paper 3 of Edexcel A-level History

Question	Marks	Marks per AO	Approximate time per question	Typical question wording
1	20	AO2: 20	45 minutes to plan and write	Assess the value of the source for revealing…
2 OR 3	20	AO1: 20	45 minutes to plan and write	How far… How accurate… To what extent… How significant…
4 OR 5	20	AO1: 20	45 minutes to read, plan and write	As for questions 2 and 3, but the questions may be comparative, turning points or patterns of change questions.

OCR
AS

All the information about this qualification can be found here: www.ocr.org.uk/qualifications/as-a-level-gce-history-a-h105-h505-from-2015/

The features of the examination

OCR AS History consists of two exam papers which are both 1 hour 30 minutes in length. There are 50 marks available in each examination, for a total of 100 marks.

Each paper covers a different area of study:

→ Unit 1 is a study of a period of **British history**, with one period chosen from a wide choice.

→ Unit 2 is a period of **European or world history**, with one period chosen from a wide choice of period from *c.*550 to 1999.

The structure of the examination

Although each examination paper consists of two sections, A and B, the nature of the questions and choice differs between Unit 1 and Unit 2.

In **Unit 1** papers there are two sections. Section A is the enquiry or source-based element of the paper. There are two compulsory questions based on three written primary sources:

→ Question 1 asks you how useful one of the sources is for studying a particular issue and is worth 10 marks.

→ Question 2 asks you to use all the sources in their historical context to assess a view about an issue and is worth 20 marks.

Section B of Unit 1 is the essay section and you have to answer either Question 3 or Question 4. The questions will ask you to assess the importance of factors, or how far you agree with a statement, or to what extent a particular issue, event or person was responsible for something. The essay is worth 20 marks.

In **Unit 2** there are two sections. Section A is the essay section and again you have to answer one question from a choice of two. The types of question asked are the same as for the Unit 1 essays. However, there are 30 marks for this section.

Section B of Unit 2 is the interpretation question. You are given an interpretation by a named historian and asked to evaluate the strengths and limitations of the interpretation by applying contextual knowledge. The interpretation is usually just one or two sentences in length. You do not have to comment about the historian or consider the provenance of the interpretation. The specification tells you from which two of the four study topics the interpretation will be chosen. The question is worth 20 marks.

Marks and time

Tables 8.10 and 8.11 show the mark allocations for the questions in the two units, along with the approximate time you should allow per question. The kinds of wording typically used in the questions are also shown.

Table 8.10 Unit 1 of OCR AS History

Question	Marks	Marks per AO	Approximate time per question	Typical question wording
1	10	AO2: 10	15 minutes to plan and write	How useful…
2	20	AO2: 20	35 minutes to plan and write	Assess how far they support the view…
3 OR 4	20	AO2: 20	40 minutes to plan and write	Assess… How far do you agree… To what extent…

Table 8.11 Unit 2 of OCR AS History

Question	Marks	Marks per AO	Approximate time per question	Typical question wording
1 OR 2	30	AO1: 30	60 minutes to plan and write	Assess… To what extent… How far do you agree…
3	20	AO3: 20	30 minutes to plan and write	Evaluate…

A-level

All the information about this qualification can be found here: www.ocr.org.uk/qualifications/as-a-level-gce-history-a-h105-h505-from-2015/

The features of the examination

OCR A-level History consists of three examination papers and a non-examined topic-based essay. Each of the examination papers is of a different length and carries a different number of marks:

→ Unit 1 is 1 hour 30 minutes long and carries 50 marks.
→ Unit 2 is 1 hour long and carries 30 marks.
→ Unit 3 is 2 hours 30 minutes long and carries 80 marks.

The non-examined topic essay carries 40 marks. This gives a total of 200 marks.

Each paper covers a different area of study:

→ Unit 1 is a study of **British history** which covers a period of approximately 50 to 100 years. You will study one period from a choice of 13.

→ Unit 2 is a study of **non-British history** which covers a period of approximately 50 to 100 years. You will study one period from a choice of 24.

→ Unit 3 is a **thematic and historical interpretation** paper which covers at least 100 years. You will study one theme from a choice of 21.

The **topic-based essay** is a non-examined unit which consists of individual research on a question that has been approved by the examination board. Using primary and secondary sources, you are required to write an essay of about 4,000 words. The essay is marked internally and moderated by the examination board.

The structure of the examination

The structure of each of the examination papers is different. Units 1 and 3 consist of two sections, A and B, while Unit 2 has just one section. The nature of the questions and choice is also different between the units.

In **Unit 1** papers there are two sections. Section A is the enquiry or source-based element of the paper. There is one compulsory question based on four written primary sources. The question asks you to use all the sources in their historical context to assess a view about an issue and is worth 30 marks.

Section B of Unit 1 is the essay section. Here you have to answer either Question 2 or Question 3. The questions will ask you to assess the importance of factors, or how far you agree with a statement, or to what extent a particular issue, event or person was responsible for something. The essay is worth 20 marks.

In **Unit 2** there is one section, and as with the essay section in Unit 1 you have to answer one question from a choice of two. However, there are two parts to each question and you must answer both. The first part is a short-answer question where you are asked to assess the importance or the significance of two events, issues or people and reach a judgement as to which is the more important. The short-answer question is worth 10 marks. The second part of the question is the long essay, similar to that in Unit 1, and is worth 20 marks.

In **Unit 3** there are two sections. Section A is the historical interpretation section. The specification provides details of the three in-depth topics associated with the theme that you are studying. You will be given two interpretations by historians on one aspect of one of the topics and asked to evaluate both interpretations by applying contextual knowledge and reach a judgement as to which is the more convincing. You will not be required to comment on the provenance of the two interpretations. The question is worth 30 marks.

In Section B of Unit 3 there will be three essay questions and you will have to answer two. Each question requires you to cover the whole period, unless you are told otherwise, and you will need to make comparisons across the period to show and explain similarities and differences, and continuity and change. Each of the essays is worth 25 marks, so this section is worth 50 marks.

The **topic-based essay** is an individual piece of research completed over the course of your study. You should write about 4,000 words in answer to your question and in this you should evaluate a range of primary sources and secondary interpretations. The essay is worth 40 marks.

Marks and time

Tables 8.12, 8.13 and 8.14 show the mark allocations for the questions in the three examined units, along with the approximate time you should allow per question. The kinds of wording typically used in the questions are also shown.

Table 8.12 Unit 1 of OCR A-level History

Question	Marks	Marks per AO	Approximate time per question	Typical question wording
1	30	AO2: 30	50 minutes including reading and planning time	Assess how far they support the view…
2 OR 3	20	AO1: 20	40 minutes including planning time	Assess… How far do you agree… To what extent…

Table 8.13 Unit 2 of OCR A-level History

Question	Marks	Marks per AO	Approximate time per question	Typical question wording
1a OR 2a	10	AO1: 10	15 minutes including planning	Explain…
1b OR 2b	20	AO1: 20	45 minutes including planning	Assess… How far do you agree… To what extent…

Table 8.14 Unit 3 of OCR A-level

Question	Marks	Marks per AO	Approximate time per question	Typical question wording
1	30	AO3: 30	1 hour including reading and planning	Evaluate…
2, 3 and 4 (choose TWO)	25 each	AO1: 25 each	45 minutes for each, including planning	Assess… How far do you agree… To what extent…

Unit 4

The topic-based essay assesses all the assessment objectives, weighted as follows:

→ AO1: 20 marks
→ AO2: 10 marks
→ AO3: 10 marks

WJEC

All the information about this qualification can be found here: www.wjec.co.uk/qualifications/history/r-history-gce-asa-from-2015/

The features of the examination

WJEC provides an A-level History specification **for teaching in schools in Wales only**.

It is a **unitised specification** which provides the opportunity to take up to 40% of the assessments at the end of the first year of study. Typically this involves taking examinations in Unit 1 and Unit 2. Some candidates may then decide to 'cash in' their marks for Unit 1 and Unit 2 to gain **an AS award.** Other candidates will continue with the qualification into a second year and take the final three units, leading to **a full A-level award.**

The WJEC A-level History qualification consists of four examination papers and a non-examined topic-based essay. Two of these examination papers (Units 1 and 2) are available to candidates at the end of the first year of their study; the other two examinations (Units 3 and 4) are terminal examinations. The non-examined assessment Unit 5 is also assessed at the end of the course.

Each of the examination papers is 90 minutes long and each carries 60 marks. The non-examined assessment unit also carries 60 marks, giving the qualification 300 marks in total.

Each unit covers a different aspect of the study of history:

→ Unit 1 is a **period study** which covers a period of approximately 100 years. You will study one period from a choice of eight.

→ Unit 2 is the first half of a **depth study** which covers a period of approximately 20 years. You will do one study in depth from a choice of eight.

→ Unit 3 is a **thematic breadth study** which covers at least 100 years. You will study one thematic breadth study from a choice of ten.

→ Unit 4 is linked with Unit 2 as you continue the second half of the depth study started in Unit 2. It also covers a period of approximately 20 years.

→ Unit 5, the non-examined assessment unit, consists of **individual research** on a question approved by WJEC. You are required to investigate an issue of historical debate, analysing and evaluating both primary and historical interpretations, and to write an essay of between 3,500 and 4,000 words.

The specification includes a rationale for the specification of topics and rules on permitted combinations (pages 15–17). These ensure that the options chosen cover at least 200 years of history and involve the study of both British and non-British history.

The structure of the examination

The structure and focus of each of the examination papers is different.

Unit 1 has two sections, A and B. Each section contains two essay-style questions and you must choose one from each. In Section

A the coverage expected in answers is 15–40 years; in Section B it is 40–80 years. Unit 1 assesses AO1 so all the questions focus on understanding historical concepts and reaching substantiated judgements. Each answer is marked out of 30.

Unit 2 has two questions which are both compulsory. Question 1 is based on three primary or contemporary sources. The question will ask you to analyse and evaluate the sources in their historical context to address a specific enquiry. This question assesses AO2 and is worth 30 marks. Question 2 is based on two extracts reflecting historical interpretations. This question will ask you to use the extracts and your own understanding of the named historical debate to assess the validity of a particular interpretation. This question assesses AO3 and is worth 30 marks.

Unit 3 has two sections, A and B. Section A contains a choice of two essay-style questions covering 20–50 years. These are on a particular theme. Section B contains one compulsory essay-style question covering at least 100 years. Unit 3 assesses AO1 so all the questions focus on understanding historical concepts and reaching substantiated judgements. Each question is marked out of 30.

Unit 4 has two sections, A and B. The question in Section A is compulsory and is based on three primary or contemporary sources. The question will ask you to analyse and evaluate the sources in their historical context to address a specific enquiry. This question assesses AO2 and is worth 30 marks. Section B contains two essay-style questions and you must choose one of these. This section assesses AO1 so both questions focus on understanding historical concepts and reaching substantiated judgements. This question is marked out of 30.

Unit 5 consists of individual research on a question that has been approved by WJEC. You are required to investigate an issue of historical debate, analysing and evaluating both primary and historical interpretations, and to write an essay of between 3,500 and 4,000 words. The extended essay is marked internally and moderated by WJEC. It assesses all three assessment objectives and is marked out of 60.

Marks and time

Tables 8.15–8.18 show the mark allocations for the questions in the four examined units, along with the approximate time you should allow per question. The kinds of wording typically used in the questions are also shown.

Table 8.15 Unit 1 of WJEC History

Question	Mark	Mark per AO	Approximate time per question	Typical question wording
1 OR 2	30	AO1: 30	45 minutes including planning time	To what extent… How far do you agree… Discuss…
3 OR 4	30	AO1: 30	45 minutes including planning time	To what extent… How far do you agree… Discuss…

Table 8.16 Unit 2 of WJEC History

Question	Mark	Mark per AO	Approximate time per question	Typical question wording
1	30	AO2: 30	45 minutes including reading and planning	Analyse and evaluate…
2	30	AO3: 30	45 minutes including reading and planning	How valid is…

Table 8.17 Unit 3 of WJEC History

Question	Mark	Mark per AO	Approximate time per question	Typical question wording
1 OR 2	30	AO1: 30	45 minutes including planning time	To what extent… How far do you agree… Discuss…
3	30	AO1: 30	45 minutes including planning time	To what extent… How far do you agree… Discuss…

Table 8.18 Unit 4 of WJEC History

Question	Mark	Mark per AO	Approximate time per question	Typical question wording
1	30	AO2: 30	45 minutes including reading and planning	Analyse and evaluate…
2 OR 3	30	AO1: 30	45 minutes including planning time	To what extent… How far do you agree… Discuss…

Unit 5

The non-examined essay assesses all the assessment objectives, weighted as follows:

→ AO1: 20 marks
→ AO2: 10 marks
→ AO3: 30 marks

✓ Exam tip

Use this chapter when you are doing essay and source questions at home or in class. Always try and stick to the suggested timings so that when it comes to the examination you are used to writing in the time allowed. It is also worth handwriting timed essays rather than word-processing them so that you get accustomed to writing legibly for long periods.

You should know

> Make sure you know how you will be assessed by your examination board and the types of questions to expect.
> Familiarise yourself with the amount of time you should spend on each type of question.
> Remember there is more information available online for each of the examination boards.

Notes